SCIENCE AND VALUES

Pittsburgh Series in
Philosophy and History
of Science

Series Editors:

Adolf Grünbaum
Larry Laudan
Nicholas Rescher
Wesley C. Salmon

SCIENCE
AND
VALUES

*The Aims of Science and
Their Role in Scientific Debate*

Larry Laudan

University of California Press
Berkeley   Los Angeles   London

University of California Press
Berkeley and Los Angeles, California

University of California Press, Ltd.
London, England

Library of Congress Cataloging in Publication Data

Laudan, Larry.
  Science and values.

  (Pittsburgh series in philosophy and history of
science ; v. 11)
  Bibliography: p. 141
  Includes index.
  1. Science—Philosophy.   I. Title.   II. Series.
Q175.L295   1984   501   84-249
ISBN 0-520-05267-6

Printed in the United States of America

1 2 3 4 5 6 7 8 9

*to my favorite geologist — who never
forgot about hard rocks*

CONTENTS

Acknowledgments   ix
Preface   xi

One   Two Puzzles about Science: Reflections on Some
          Crises in Philosophy and Sociology of Science   1

          The Consensual View and the Puzzle of
              Agreement   3
          The "New Wave" Preoccupation with
              Dissensus   13

Two   The Hierarchical Structure of Scientific Debates   23

          Factual Consensus Formation   26
          Methodological Consensus Formation   33

Three   Closing the Evaluative Circle: Resolving
          Disagreements about Cognitive Values   42

          The Covariance Fallacy   43
          The Reticulated Model and the Mechanics
              of Goal Evaluation   50
          The Reticulated Model of Scientific
              Rationality   62

Four   Dissecting the Holist Picture of Scientific
          Change   67

Kuhn on the Units of Scientific Change   68
Kuhn's Critique of Methodology   87

Five   A Reticulational Critique of Realist Axiology
            and Methodology   103

Epilogue   138
References   141
Index   145

ACKNOWLEDGMENTS

Attempting to recognize one's intellectual debts is always a precarious business. The success of the enterprise rests on the monumentally implausible assumption that one can consciously recognize at the time, and is later in a position to recall, the multitude of ideas and arguments that shaped one's approach to a topic. (Not for nothing is oral history in disrepute!) There are several possible *aides de mémoire* which authors fall back on. One can record the names of one's teachers, or the authors in one's library, or one's immediate colleagues.

My own preference in these matters is to localize my obligations using a different criterion. My clear and obvious debt, at least as I see it, is to those friends and colleagues who have read and commented on all (or portions) of this essay. Their criticisms have saved me from some egregious mistakes and their encouragement has sustained me through periods when I was convinced that I had nothing fresh to say. It is their names that belong here, for this essay reflects their efforts just as much as my own.

Accordingly, I want to thank all the following heartily for the role they have played in putting this work together: Paul Anderson, Peter Barker, Benjamin Bart, Henry Bauer, Gerd Buchdahl, Richard Burian, Robert Butts, Richard Creath, Arthur Donovan, Gerald Doppelt, Maurice Finocchiaro, Arthur Fine, Ron Giere, Clark Glymour, Adolf Grünbaum, Gary Gutting, Carl Hempel, David Hull, Noretta Koertge, Rachel Laudan, Jarrett Leplin, Andrew Lugg, Ernan McMullin, Ilkka Niiniluoto, Joseph Pitt, Nicholas Rescher, Alex Rosenberg, Eleanore

Stump, Roberto Toretti, Stephen Turner, Robert Westman, John Worrall, and Steve Wykstra.

Thanks of a different sort must go to the National Science Foundation and the National Endowment for the Humanities, whose Sustained Development Grant gave me the material support necessary to see this project through to completion. Equally, my thanks go to Becky Cox, who has nurtured this manuscript through more redactions than either of us cares to remember.

One final remark is in order. This book has been several years in the making. By way of getting preliminary reactions to some of its central ideas, I published early versions of sections of chapters 1 and 5 in *Minerva* and in *Philosophy of Science*. I want to record my thanks to the editors of those journals for permission to utilize some of that material here.

Blacksburg, Virginia
15 July 1983

PREFACE

Book titles can be enormously misleading. The reader of this work, on pulling it off the shelf for the first time, may well expect from the spine to see me grappling with vexed questions about the relations between science and ethics. He may even imagine that this essay is one more contribution to the burgeoning, and decidedly second-rate, literature that agonizes over the ethical dilemmas posed by a science and technology widely, if probably wrongly, perceived to be running out of control. Let me quickly set the record straight by stating quite clearly that this book is neither about how to make scientists more moral nor about how to make moral theory more scientific, however desirable at least one of those outcomes might be.

It fails to be the one because I am under no illusions that I could tell scientists anything about the morality of their research which they do not already know; it is not the other because, although it is devoutly to be wished that moral philosophers knew more than they do about science, I would not know how to recognize a scientific ethics if I were confronted by one.[1] These are doubtless splendid topics, but they happen not to be my topics. My concern in this book is not with moral values, but with cognitive ones; not with ethical norms and rules of conduct, but with methodological norms and rules.[2] The fact that

1. I have tried to explain why in Laudan, 1982.
2. The question of precisely how one distinguishes cognitive values or aims from noncognitive ones is quite complex. For purposes of my analysis here, we can adopt

many readers will probably expect the book to be about ethical rather than cognitive values stands as eloquent testimony to the fact that, for much too long, we have imagined that the only really deep value questions that arise in, and about, science have to do with ethical or moral values. In this book I talk quite a lot about values, and to that extent its title is apt; but I have nothing to say about ethical values as such, for they are manifestly not the predominant values in the scientific enterprise. Not that ethics plays no role in science; on the contrary, ethical values are always present in scientific decision making and, very occasionally, their influence is of great importance. But that importance fades into insignificance when compared with the ubiquitous role of cognitive values. One function of this book is to redress the imbalance that has led so many recent writers on science to be preoccupied with scientific morality rather than with scientific rationality, which is more centrally my focus.

In sum, this is a book about the role of cognitive values in the shaping of scientific rationality. Among recent writers, no one has done more to direct our attention to the role of cognitive standards and values in science than Thomas Kuhn. Indeed, for more than two decades, the views of Thomas Kuhn — and reactions to them — have occupied center stage in accounts of scientific change and scientific rationality. That is as it should be, for Kuhn's *Structure of Scientific Revolutions* caused us all to rethink our image of what science is and how it works. There can be no one active today in philosophy, history, or sociology of science whose approach to the problem of scientific rationality has not been shaped by the Gestalt switch Kuhn wrought on our perspective on science. This debt is so broadly recognized that there is no need to document it here.[3] Less frequently admitted is the fact that, in the twenty-two years since the appearance of *The Structure of Scientific Revolutions,* a great deal of historical scholarship and analytic spadework has moved our understanding of the processes of scientific rationality and scientific change considerably beyond the point where Kuhn left it.

Indeed, we are now in a position to state pretty unequivocally that

---

this rough-and-ready characterization: an attribute will count as a cognitive value or aim if that attribute represents a property of theories which we deem to be constitutive of "good science."

3. One indication of the magnitude of that debt may be found by perusing Gutting, 1980.

Kuhn's model of scientific change, as developed in *Structure* and elaborated in *The Essential Tension,* is deeply flawed, not only in its specifics but in its central framework assumptions. It is thus time to acknowledge that, for all its pioneering virtue, Kuhn's *Structure* ought no longer be regarded as the *locus classicus,* the origin and fount, for treatments of these questions. It is time to say so publicly and openly, lest that larger community of scientists and interested laymen, who have neither the time nor the inclination to follow the esoteric technical literature of these fields, continues to imagine that Kuhn's writings represent the last (or at least the latest) word on these matters.

But just saying so is not enough. The decanonization of a discipline's patron saints is always a slow and arduous task, and one demanding that the case be carefully constructed and that it cut to the heart of the matter. This book is a contribution to that effort. So as not to have my intentions mistaken, let me stress that I did not set out to debunk Kuhn. My central concern in writing this essay has been from the outset to offer an account of scientific debate and scientific decision making that does as much justice as I can to what we have come to learn about how science works. Yet over and over again in that process, I have found myself denying theses and doctrines that many people (although usually not Kuhn himself, who tended to be rather tentative in his claims) regard Kuhn as having decisively established. For that reason, if for no other, Kuhn—or what Kuhn has been made into by his expositors—stalks the pages of this work as a presence to be both acknowledged and ultimately exorcised. Yet that is surely the wrong image. No one working in this field in this generation can get Kuhn entirely out of his system. Nor should we try, for he has posed an impressive range of important and fertile questions. What we can demand is that we honestly face up to the fact that his answers to most of those questions, never fully compelling, are no longer even plausible.

This book purports to provide better answers to some of Kuhn's questions than Kuhn himself did, and to diagnose why Kuhn, along with such fellow travelers as Feyerabend and Hanson, was never able to produce answers as compelling as his questions. There is no particular hubris involved in making that claim; indeed, something would be dreadfully wrong if, two decades after the appearance of Kuhn's masterpiece, one were not able to sustain such a claim. There is progress in philosophy just as surely as, if more slowly than, there is in science; although Kuhn himself, ever a believer in a sharp demarcation between science and everything else, might well dispute it. In any event, it is not in my power, nor is it my intention, to detract from Kuhn's seminal contribution when I assert that we have by now built upon it and moved beyond it. It is the burden of the arguments in the chapters that follow to show why that is the proper thing to say.

Chapter One

TWO PUZZLES ABOUT SCIENCE: REFLECTIONS ON SOME CRISES IN PHILOSOPHY AND SOCIOLOGY OF SCIENCE

Science has posed a plethora of interesting challenges to several of the major philosophers and sociologists of the past half century. Indeed, trying to understand and to explain the workings of science has preoccupied several of the leading thinkers in these otherwise disparate fields. This book is an effort to help resolve a few of those challenges. But before I can expect my solutions to be taken seriously, I need to show that the problems I am grappling with are both real and as yet unresolved. I know no better way of motivating problems than by a brief survey of their recent history, a history that, in this particular instance, involves some intriguing intersections between the concerns of philosophers and sociologists.

During the 1940s and 1950s each of these disciplines developed and elaborated its own picture of how science behaves. The philosophical accounts I have in mind are those of the logical empiricists and Popper; the sociological model is associated chiefly with Merton and his followers. Although there were important differences of emphasis between the philosophical and sociological accounts of science offered by scholars of that generation, their respective pictures—now that we have some distance from them—appear to be quite similar and decidedly complementary. These similarities are less surprising than they might initially appear because, despite occasional outbreaks of rivalry between the two disciplines, both sociologists and philosophers of that era shared a basic premise and a common problem. The premise was that science is culturally unique and to be demarcated sharply from other intellectual pursuits such as philosophy, theology, and aesthetics.[1] The central problem each sought to explain was the impressively high degree of agreement in science. During the 1960s and 1970s, however, the views on these matters held by many sociologists and philosophers of science began to undergo transformation. Gone, or in serious disarray, by the mid-1970s were most of the familiar theses of logical empiricism and Mertonian sociology. In their place came accounts of science radically at odds with their predecessors. But if the newer analyses differed sharply from the old (in ways to be described below), there were still intriguing consiliences between the new philosophical and the new sociological perspectives on science. Chief among these points of common interest shared by "new-wave" accounts of science was a conviction that the central intellectual puzzle about science required explaining the periodic outbursts of disagreement in science.

In a nutshell, students of the development of science, whether sociologists or philosophers, have alternately been preoccupied with explaining consensus in science or with highlighting disagreement and divergence. Those contrasting focuses would be harmless if all they represented were differences of emphasis or interest. After all, no one can fix simultaneously on all sides of any question. What creates the tension is that neither approach has shown itself to have the explanatory resources for dealing with both. More specifically, as we shall see, whatever success can be claimed by each of these models in explaining its own preferred problem is largely negated by its inability to grapple with the core problem of its rivals. Thus, the sociological and philosophical models of science of the 1940s and 1950s adopt such strong assumptions about the consensus-forming mechanisms they postulate to explain agreement that it is difficult to make much sense of the range and character of scientific disagreements and controversies. The more recent models, for all their promise of revealing the manifold

---

1. Recall, for instance, Karl Popper's remarkable claim dating from this period that the most important task of epistemology was to demarcate between science and nonscience.

reasons why scientists might agree to differ, leave us largely in the dark about how scientists could ever reasonably resolve their differences in the definitive fashion in which they often do terminate controversies.

The theme of this essay, in its starkest form, is simply (*a*) that existing accounts lack the explanatory resources to tackle these two puzzles in tandem; (*b*) that this is especially true of several recently fashionable approaches to science, which turn out to be at least as flawed as those they would replace; and (*c*) that we need a single, unified theory of scientific rationality which promises to be able to explain both these striking features about science. My aim in this first chapter is to diagnose how we landed in the mess of being able to explain one or the other of these puzzles, but not both. The remainder of the book delineates some machinery that explains how both consensus and dissensus can arise, and how each can sometimes give rise to the other.

THE CONSENSUAL VIEW AND THE
PUZZLE OF AGREEMENT

To anyone working in the humanities or the social sciences, where debate and disagreement between rival factions are pandemic, the natural sciences present a tranquil scene indeed. For the most part, natural scientists working in any field or subfield tend to be in agreement about most of the assertions of their discipline. They will typically agree about many of the central phenomena to be explained and about the broad range of quantitative and experimental techniques appropriate for establishing "factual claims." Beyond this agreement about what is to be explained, there is usually agreement at the deeper level of explanatory and theoretical entities. Chemists, for instance, talk quite happily about atomic structure and subatomic particles. Geologists, at least for now, treat in a matter-of-fact fashion claims about the existence of massive subterranean plates whose motion is thought to produce most of the observable (i.e., surface) tectonic activity—claims that, three decades ago, would have been treated as hopelessly speculative. Biologists agree about the general structure of DNA and about many of the general mechanisms of evolution, even though few can be directly observed. One intuitive yardstick of this staggering degree of agreement emerges from a comparison of science textbooks with texts in, say, philosophy or sociology. (And such comparisons are to the point since it was primarily sociologists and philosophers who, looking carefully at science, were struck by its comparatively high degree of consensus.) Philosophers are notorious for debating fundamentals and there is little agreement between the rival schools or factions of philosophy on anything, not even on which problems are of central importance to the discipline. So it comes as no surprise that philosophy texts written by (say) Thomists have precious little in common with those written by positivists. Similarly, sociology is divided into numerous warring camps, to such a degree that there are glaring divergences among sociology textbooks produced by (say) Marxists, hermeneutists, phenomenologists, functionalists, or sociometricians. Each school of philosophy or sociology offers a fundamentally different agenda of central issues for the field, and each advocates rather different methods for testing or evaluating disciplinary claims. The natural sciences are simply not like that, or at least so many sociologists and philosophers of the 1950s and 1960s surmised.

So impressed were many philosophers and sociologists by the extent of agreement in science that they often took that degree of agreement to be the central, even the defining, epistemic and cognitive feature of science. The well-known philosopher of science, N. R. Campbell, puts it quite bluntly: "Science *is* the study of those judgments concerning which universal agreement can be reached."[2] Speaking for the sociologists, John Ziman concurs: "[Consensus] is the basic principle upon which science is founded. It is not a subsidiary consequence of the 'scientific method.' It is the Scientific Method itself."[3]

What makes the broad degree of agreement in science even more perplexing is the fact that the theories around which consensus forms do themselves rapidly come and go. The high degree of agreement which characterizes science might be less surprising if science, like some monastic religions, had settled upon a body of doctrine which was to be its permanent dogma. Consensus, once reached in those circumstances, might well be expected to sustain itself for a long period of time. But science offers us the remarkable spectacle of a discipline in which older views on many central issues are rapidly and frequently displaced by newer ones, and where nonetheless most members of the scientific community will change horses in midstream to embrace a

2. Campbell, 1952, p. 27. Elsewhere, Campbell wrote: "The subject matter of science consists of those judgements for which universal assent can be obtained" (1957, p. 22).

3. Ziman, 1968, p. 9.

point of view which may never even have been mooted a decade earlier. Moreover, change occurs at a variety of levels. Some of the central problems of the discipline change; the basic explanatory hypotheses shift; and even the rules of investigation slowly evolve. That a consensus can be shaped and reshaped amid such flux is indeed remarkable. However unsatisfactory the models of scientific consensus offered by the last generation may now appear to be, it is surely easy enough to understand why their framers believed that the explanation of scientific agreement must be a central consideration for any theory about how science works. For, when one takes into account the rapid-fire manner in which new views emerge, the staggering thing about science is not that consensus is generally reached so quickly and with such unanimity; what is astounding is that consensus is ever reached at all.

Taking the high level of consensus in science as a datum, intellectuals of the preceding generation constructed models of science, and especially of scientific decision making, which were designed to explain how science differed structurally and methodologically from such ideology-laden fields as social and political theory or metaphysics. I want to describe the salient features of some of those models, for an appreciation of their strengths and weaknesses will be useful later on.

a) Philosophers and consensus. — Philosophers of the 1930s and 1940s, turning anew to science after a generation of comparative philosophical neglect by many idealists and Neo-Kantians in the first decades of the twentieth century, already had some sophisticated machinery in their kits for explaining how science could be a consensual activity. Indeed, for a very long time philosophers generally have been inclined to accept what I call the Leibnizian ideal. In brief, the Leibnizian ideal holds that all disputes about matters of fact can be impartially resolved by invoking appropriate rules of evidence. At least since Bacon, most philosophers have believed there to be an algorithm or set of algorithms which would permit any impartial observer to judge the degree to which a certain body of data rendered different explanations of those data true or false, probable or improbable. Philosophers have expressed varying degrees of optimism about whether we now know precisely what those evidentiary rules are. (Mill, for instance, believed that we already had them in hand. Others, more pessimistic, believed that we had yet to develop the full kit.) But whether optimist or pessimist, rationalist or empiricist, most logicians and philosophers of science from the 1930s through the 1950s believed, at least in principle, in the Leibnizian ideal. That they did so had immediate relevance to their views about consensus in science, for science was regarded as consisting entirely in claims about matters of fact. Since scientific disagreements were thought to be, at bottom, disagreements about matters of fact, and since disagreements of that sort were thought to be mechanically resolvable, philosophers had a ready sketch of an explanation for consensus formation in science.

Specifically, they argued that there are rules of scientific methodology which are responsible for producing consensus in a rational community such as science was thought to be. If scientists disagree about the merits of two rival theories, they need only consult the appropriate rules of evidence to see which theory is better supported. Should those rules fail to decide the issue immediately (e.g., should both theories prove to be equally well supported by the available data), then all that was required to terminate disagreement was the collection of new and more discriminating evidence which would differentially confirm or disconfirm one of the theories under consideration. In this view of the matter, scientific disagreement was invariably transitory and unstable. Disagreements about the facts could arise among rational men only when the evidence in a particular domain was relatively thin or incomplete. Once identified, the disagreement could be brought to rational closure by collecting more evidence and by insisting on following the appropriate rules for assessing evidential support. In sum, philosophers preached that science was a consensual activity because scientists (insofar as they were rational) shaped their beliefs, implicitly if not explicitly, according to the canons of a shared "scientific methodology" or "inductive logic," and those canons were thought to be more than sufficient to resolve any genuine disagreement about matters of fact. To this end, many prominent philosophers of science of this period (e.g., Carnap, Reichenbach, and Popper) saw their primary task to be precisely that of explicating the rules of evidential inference which scientists use implicitly in making theory choices.

This explanation of scientific consensus had some very tempting features. In the first place, it accorded neatly with the account that scientists themselves were prone to give of their activity. For decades, scientists had been extolling the virtues of the scientific method and they tended, like the philosophers, to see that method as the engine driving scientists to agreement. This approach also represented the traditional philosophical wisdom in these matters, since regarding science as a rule-governed activity for the generation of beliefs about the physical world had long been the norm among philosophers.

During the 1940s and 1950s, then, most philosophers of science were of one mind in holding that science was characterized cognitively chiefly by its high level of agreement and also in attributing that degree of consensus to the willingness of scientists to submit their opinions to arbitration by an impartial logic of theory appraisal. If there were any nagging worries to upset this picture, they chiefly grew out of the fact that, as many philosophers knew, scientific disagreements did not always or quickly evaporate in the face of new and discriminating evidence. After all, Copernicans and Ptolemaists fought it out for well over a century. Advocates of the wave and particle theories of light were at loggerheads for half of the nineteenth century. Pro- and anti-atomists churned up physics and chemistry more or less steadily from Dalton's *New System of Chemistry* (1810) until the beginning of the twentieth century. The existence of such long-term controversies in science, even recent science, did not by itself refute the Leibnizian ideal, as several face-saving options were open to its defenders. For instance, one could, and some did, argue that scientists are sometimes irrational in the face of the evidence and refuse to recognize the better theory. Such labels were frequently applied, for instance, to Priestley and the phlogistonists or to the opponents of atomism or to the post-Copernican followers of Ptolemy.

If the persistence of some controversies could be attributed to the stubbornness of scientists rather than to the indeterminacy of the rules for theory choice, then the Leibnizian ideal continued to look attractive. Alternatively, and more commonly, it was open to defenders of the Leibnizian ideal to suggest that these long-term controversies were merely *querelles de mots*. According to this view, there was no real difference between the theories of the contending parties (i.e., the theories were empirically equivalent); the disputes persisted only because the contenders failed to recognize the equivalence of their models. Precisely this view was taken in the 1950s by a number of philosophers and historians with respect, for instance, to explaining the prolonged debate between the Ptolemaic and Copernican hypotheses.[4] Elaborate proofs were set out to show that the two systems were "observationally equivalent"; the latent function of these proofs was apparently to show

4. See, for instance, Price, 1959.

that this long-standing controversy was not the refutation of the reigning consensual models and the Leibnizian ideal which it appeared to
be. Similar claims were made about the observational equivalence of
matrix and wave mechanics and about corpuscular and wave optics.
(As we now know, most of these arguments were bogus, for they depended on showing that two theories were equivalent so long as their
formal structures—i.e., their mathematical representations—could be
shown to be homologous. Unfortunately, these proofs of "empirical
equivalence" work only if we divest these theories of most of their substantive claims. But more of that in chapter 5 below.) Thus the philosophical advocates of consensus as the scientific norm could explain
away the apparent exceptions to that consensus by insisting that, when
consensus was not reached as quickly as one might expect, it was either
because the decisive evidence was not sought, or because the scientists
concerned did not realize that their rival theories really amounted to
the same thing, or (in the last resort) because scientists were not behav-
ing rationally.

Other prominent elements of the philosophy of science of logical
empiricism contributed to the impression that science should indeed
be a consensual activity. It was commonly asserted, for instance, that
one core rule of scientific method was that acceptable new theories
must be able to explain all the successes of their predecessors and some
new facts as well. Science, in short, was thought to be strictly cumulative. With this strong constraint in place, it became possible to explain
how scientific change could be effected fairly quickly. After all, if a
new theory emerged which managed to account for everything its
predecessor could, and some other things besides, then it would seem
that no sensible person could resist the appeal of the new theory. So
long as theory change could be said to be strictly cumulative, the philosopher had a ready explanation for the staggeringly swift changes of
loyalty which accompany many so-called scientific revolutions. And it
is for just this reason that the post-1960s discovery that theory change
in science is generally noncumulative and nonconvergent created such
acute difficulties for the logical empiricists and for Popper.[5]

b) *Sociologists and scientific consensus.* — If philosophers had a long
tradition of expecting and explaining the existence of agreement about

---

5. For a fuller discussion of the significance of the noncumulativity of scientific
theories, see chapter 5 below.

matters of fact, sociologists did not. Indeed, prior to the 1930s there scarcely was a sociology of science worthy of the name. The following two decades, however, saw a significant flowering of sociological studies of science. Central to much of the research of that era are our dual problems of consensus and dissensus. As with the philosophers, sociologists tended to regard the former as the natural state of the physical sciences, whereas the latter required special explanation as a deviation from the expected norm.

Whereas philosophers located the source of the consensual character of science in the scientist's adherence to the canons of a logic of scientific inference, sociologists argued that science exhibited so high a degree of agreement because scientists shared a set of norms or standards which governed the professional life of the scientific community. Robert Merton, for instance, argued that scientific subcultures shared the norms of "universalism, communism, disinterestedness, and organized scepticism."[6] These norms, which are "held to be binding on the man of science, . . . are expressed in the form of prescriptions, proscriptions, preferences and permissions."[7] It is, in short, because scientists share the same values or standards that they are able to form stable patterns of consensus. Merton was later to find what he regarded as strong support for the hypothesis of shared scientific norms and standards in research he did with Harriet Zuckerman. Specifically, he and Zuckerman discovered that journals in the humanities and social sciences have a consistently higher rejection rate for submitted articles than do journals in the natural sciences. (In the Merton and Zuckerman study, for instance, the physics journals sampled rejected only 24 percent of submissions, whereas sociology and philosophy journals rejected more than 80 percent.) Merton took these divergences as evidence that philosophers and sociologists could not agree about what constituted significant or solid research, whereas natural scientists could agree about the merits of specific contributions by virtue of their shared norms and values. As Merton and Zuckerman wrote in 1971, "This suggests that these fields of learning [i.e., sociology and philosophy] are not greatly institutionalized in the reasonably precise sense that editors and referees on the one side and would-be contributors on

6. For a detailed account of these norms, see Merton's classic "The Normative Structure of Science," reprinted in Merton, 1973.
7. Merton, 1973, pp. 268-269.

the other almost always share norms of what constitutes adequate scholarship."[8] In sum, the review process in science, along with other features of its reward system, manages to institutionalize and to internalize the professional norms far more successfully (i.e., more uniformly) than the nonsciences do. The norms of science are not always explicit, but Merton is convinced that they are always decisive: "It has become manifest that in each age there is a system of science that rests upon a set of [normative] assumptions, usually implicit and seldom questioned by most scientific workers of the time."[9] Twenty years earlier Michael Polanyi had sketched a similar explanation for the high degree of consensus in science. "Each [scientist]," he wrote, "is pursuing a common underlying purpose and . . . each can sufficiently judge — in general accordance with other scientific opinion — whether his contribution is valid or not."[10] In Polanyi's view, this internalization of shared norms or standards explains the "spontaneous co-ordination [i.e., agreement] of scientists."[11]

No more than their philosophical counterparts did sociologists of this period think that agreement in science was inevitable or ubiquitous. They knew, of course, about some of the famous scientific controversies that have divided the scientific community into warring factions. But sociologists, such as Merton and his colleague Bernard Barber, tended to explain these deviations from the expected consensus by arguing that "prejudice and superstition" could sometimes serve as institutional and intellectual obstacles to scientists following the "scientific" norms expected of them. Barber, in particular, argued at length in a much cited study that philosophy and theology have sometimes intruded into science, making it difficult if not impossible for scientists to adhere conscientiously to their professional norms.[12] Thus, if it seems odd from a consensualist perspective that astronomers, supposedly sharing the same norms, should disagree for a century and a half about the merits of Ptolemy and Copernicus, then a sociologist of this persuasion accounts for that controversy by conjecturing that the

8. Ibid., p. 472. Still later in this essay, Merton makes the claim even more explicit: "the marked differences in rejection rates of journals in the various disciplines can be tentatively ascribed . . . in part to differences in the extent of consensus with regard to standards of adequate science and scholarship" (p. 474).

9. Ibid., p. 250.

10. Polanyi, 1951, p. 39.

11. Merton, 1973, pp. 268-269.

12. See especially Barber, 1961.

followers of Ptolemy were religiously prejudiced men who had only partly internalized the appropriate norms of science. The Copernicans, so the explanation goes, more fully succeeded in acting as scientists because they managed to separate secular and sectarian values. As quaint as these explanations now appear (for few historians of science would still venture to claim either that Ptolemaists were less scientific than Copernicus or that Copernicus was less "metaphysical" than Ptolemy), such explanations were commonplace throughout the 1940s and 1950s, and they went largely unchallenged by the sociologists and philosophers of the period. What is important for our purposes is that the sociological advocates of these consensualist approaches were convinced that, once the appropriate scientific norms did reassert themselves, scientific controversies would come to a decisive end. To this extent they accepted a sociologized version of the Leibnizian ideal, albeit one in which shared values, institutionalized into a collective system of rewards and punishment — rather than a methodological algorithm — provided the alchemy needed to bring harmony out of disagreement.

Rarely does Merton specifically say that the shared norms that guide and direct scientific research are the same norms that his philosophical contemporaries were taking to be constitutive of the scientific method, although he does write that "the institutional imperatives [or norms] derive from the goal and methods [of science]."[13] But it is not crucial for my purposes to insist on a virtual identity between the philosophical and sociological accounts of science dating from this period. What should be clear, however, is that both sociologists and philosophers of that era were inclined to think that agreement among scientists about the "facts of the matter" was the natural state of affairs and were disposed to explain such factual agreement by insisting that it was the direct result of agreement among scientists at a "deeper" level — at the level of procedures and methods (as the philosophers would put it) or at the level of norms and standards, incorporated into an institutional reward system (as the sociologists would have it). Both camps insisted that scientific agreement was the by-product of a prior methodological

13. Merton, 1973, p. 270. As further evidence that Merton believed that the norms were ultimately grounded in the rules of method, consider that he defines one of the core norms, organized skepticism, as "the detached scrutiny of beliefs in terms of empirical and logical criteria" (Merton, 1968, chap. 8). Such criteria are surely those provided by the rules of scientific methodology.

and axiological compact. In Polanyi's words, "the consensus of scientific opinion" changes because each of the various groups in science "agrees with respect to their standards."[14] What was said to make scientists unique, and to explain their near unanimity on most matters of fact, was a more fundamental consensus about the guiding aims of the activity and about the most effective means of implementing those ends.

As we now know, the consensual view of philosophers and sociologists of the 1950s and 1960s will not stand up to sustained analysis. Scientists have disagreed far too often and about too many important matters for one to treat scientific disagreements as minor deviations from a consensual norm. More to the point, we have studied many of these disagreements in sufficient detail to see that the explanatory resources of classical philosophy and sociology of science are impotent to handle the broad range of cases in which disagreement arises. It is frequently true, for instance, that scientists who are doing their best to follow appropriate norms of disinterestedness, objectivity, and rationality nonetheless find themselves led to very divergent conclusions. We now understand how deeply the data in science, especially at the research frontier, can underdetermine choice between theories. We now know that the logical empiricists were simply wrong in believing that all scientists have subscribed to the same methodological and evaluative standards. We have been able to show over and again that the prolonged scientific disagreements of the past were not mere *querrelles de mots* between empirically equivalent theories, but were, rather, genuine controversies between profoundly different rival frameworks which appeared, for a time, to be equally well supported by the available evidence.[15] Much information has accumulated in the past decade to suggest that scientists often violate Merton's proposed norms for scientific behavior and, on occasion, are even rewarded for such violations. More tellingly, we can easily specify circumstances in which a willingness to break with those norms is important for the progress of science.

That said, we ought not conclude that there is nothing right in the analysis of the logical empiricists and the Mertonians. As we shall see later, these scholars put their finger on important features of the scientific enterprise. But what can be added with some conviction is that

14. Polanyi, 1951, p. 217.
15. For a discussion of the groundlessness of many attempts to reduce genuine disagreements to mere verbal disputes, see Laudan, 1968; 1977, chap. 2.

neither approach has shown itself to have the explanatory resources to account for disagreement of the degree and of the kind which science, past as well as present, produces in abundance. As scholars began to discover some of the flaws in, and exceptions to, these earlier models, they reacted in a not uncommon way by suggesting that we must start again from scratch, more or less repudiating everything in the prevailing but discredited paradigm. Writers like Kuhn, Feyerabend, and a host of younger sociologists of science have spent the past several years developing an explanation of dissensus in science. It is to some of those models that I now turn.

THE "NEW-WAVE" PREOCCUPATION WITH DISSENSUS

To make a long story short, there are four lines of argument which undermine the classical preoccupation with scientific consensus: the discovery that scientific research is much more controversy-laden than the older view would lead one to expect; the thesis of theory incommensurability; the thesis of the underdetermination of theories; and the phenomenon of successful counternormal behavior. I want to discuss each of these matters briefly.

a) The ubiquity of controversy. — Theories change rapidly in science; it is a cliché that yesterday's science fiction becomes today's scientific orthodoxy. But sometimes these changes can turn into drawn-out, vituperative affairs that introduce fundamental divisions of belief and loyalty within the scientific community. I have already mentioned a few such debates: Copernicus-Ptolemy, wave-particle optics, atomism versus energetics. The list can be extended more or less indefinitely to include Newtonian versus Cartesian mechanics, uniformitarian versus catastrophist geology, vis viva versus momentum mechanics, one-versus two-fluid theories of electricity, Priestley versus Lavoisier in chemistry, the debates about spontaneous generation, Einstein versus Bohr on quantum mechanics, special creation versus evolutionary biology, the recent debates about continental drift, and so on. Each involved prominent scientists on both sides, genuinely different theories, lasted several decades, and seemed to count reasonable arguments on both sides. Cases such as these seem to make it clear that, whatever force the rules and norms of science may have going for them, they were in fact insufficient to bring these controversies quickly to a definitive resolution.

There is a different way in which one may formulate the point. If the consensual model and its implied Leibnizian ideal were sound, it is very difficult to understand how mavericks or revolutionaries in the scientific community could ever get their ideas off the ground. As Kuhn cogently argued, "In short, if a new candidate for [reigning] paradigm had to be judged from the start by hard-headed people who examined only relative problem-solving ability, the sciences would experience very few major revolutions."[16] Since revolutions do not occur overnight, every scientific revolution must be inaugurated by a period when some scientists are pursuing new ideas and others are quite happy with the reigning theories. The consensual model was said by its critics to make it very difficult to understand how reasonable men could ever differ, in ways that seem to be required to permit the exploration of new ideas. As Thomas Kuhn succinctly formulated this objection to the consensual approach: the emergence of new scientific ideas *"requires* a decision process which permits rational men to disagree, and such disagreement would generally be barred by the shared algorithm which philosophers have generally sought. If it [i.e., such an algorithm] were at hand, all conforming [i.e., rational] scientists would make the same decision at the same time."[17] Kuhn maintains that it is only the existence of differential preferences and values among scientists which allows new theories to flower. Otherwise, "no one . . . would be inclined to try out the new theory, to articulate it in ways which showed its fruitfulness or displayed its accuracy and scope."[18] It is telling that Kuhn in this passage, as in much of his work, ignores the fact that scientists can distinguish between criteria for acceptance of theories and criteria of pursuit worthiness.[19] Such a distinction allows one to circumvent some of the problems Kuhn raises for the consensual view. But to this extent Kuhn is surely right: the consensual view fails to make sense of the broad range and variety of cases of scientific disagreement. Because it does, something more must be going on than meets the consensual eye.

   b) The thesis of incommensurability. — Kuhn himself proposed to fill in a part of the picture by claiming that the advocates of rival theories simply fail to communicate with one another. This failure is no

16. Kuhn, 1962, p. 156.
17. Kuhn, 1977 (italics in original).
18. Ibid., p. 332.
19. For a lengthy discussion of the difference between acceptance and pursuit, see Laudan, 1977, chap. 4.

accident, he thinks, because rival theories are radically incommensurable. We can see why he thinks so by looking at Kuhn's account of interparadigmatic disagreement. Far more than many of his predecessors, Kuhn was cognizant of the extent to which the history of science was rife with major controversies. He had himself written a very influential book about one such controversy, *The Copernican Revolution.* As Kuhn saw it, periods of scientific revolution were characterized by the (unpeaceful) coexistence of a variety of rival paradigms or world views, each with its own advocates. As Kuhn described these clashes between rival paradigms, they were always inconclusive. This is because the paradigms themselves were "incommensurable." Advocates of one paradigm literally could not understand their rivals; they lived in different worlds. They might use the same terminology, but they would typically mean fundamentally different things by it. The impossibility of full translation between rival paradigms is further exacerbated by the fact that, as Kuhn claims in his more recent *The Essential Tension,* the advocates of different paradigms often subscribe to different methodological standards and have nonidentical sets of cognitive values. Thus, what one party to a dispute views as a positive attribute in a theory may well be viewed as a liability by advocates of a different paradigm. So, there is a failure of communication with respect to both the substance of theories and the standards regarded as appropriate for their appraisal.

c) The underdetermination of theories by data. — Probably more important than either of the previous nudges toward a focus on disagreement was a family of arguments concerning underdetermination. In brief, they amount to the claim that the rules or evaluative criteria of science do not pick out one theory uniquely or unambiguously to the exclusion of all its contraries. Several separate lines of argument lead to this conclusion. One is the so-called Duheim-Quine thesis, according to which no theory can be logically proved or refuted by any body of evidence. Another route to the same conclusion hinges on the claim (associated, for rather different reasons, with the work of Wittgenstein and Nelson Goodman) that the rules of scientific inference, whether deductive or inductive, are so radically ambiguous that they can be followed in indefinitely many, mutually inconsistent ways. Pursuing a similar line, Kuhn has argued (in *The Essential Tension*) that the criteria of theory choice shared by scientists are too ambiguous to determine choice. This cluster of arguments has often been taken to entail that science cannot be the rule-governed activity that many empiricists and sociologists made it out to be.

d) Counternormal behavior. — Paul Feyerabend and Ian Mitroff have both argued that many highly successful scientists have repeatedly violated the norms or canons usually called scientific.[20] From time to time, scientists have ignored the evidence, tolerated inconsistencies, and pursued counterinductive strategies. More to the point, many of the most noteworthy instances of scientific progress seem to have involved scientists who rode roughshod over conventional methodological sensibilities. Minimally, such behavior seems to suggest (as Mitroff argues) that Merton has misidentified the norms that guide scientific practice. More radically, such behavior might lead one to conclude with Feyerabend that, where methods are concerned, "anything goes."

With such ammunition in hand, new-wave sociologists and philosophers of the last ten or fifteen years have been urging us to focus chiefly on scientific debate and disagreement, for (as they see it) such disagreement is far more likely to be the "natural" state of science than consensus is. More than that, these scholars have laid out elaborate machinery for explaining how disagreement could arise and persist (e.g., from incommensurability or underdetermination). But, as I have already hinted, these writers are ill equipped to explain how agreement ever congeals. To see how this approach comes unstuck with the problem of consensus formation, let us consider in some detail the difficulties that agreement poses for Kuhn's analysis. Because he believes that interparadigmatic dialogue is inevitably partial and incomplete, and because he thinks that the partisans of different paradigms subscribe to different methodological standards, Kuhn can readily explain why many scientific debates are protracted and inconclusive affairs. If both sides are indeed "talking past one another," if they are judging their theories against different yardsticks, then it is no surprise that they continue to disagree. In sum, Kuhn's model correctly predicts that dissensus should be a common feature of scientific life. What it cannot explain so readily, if at all, is how—short of sheer exhaustion or political manipulation—scientific disagreements are ever brought to closure. If rival scientists cannot understand one another's point of view, if they have fundamentally different expectations

---

20. See Feyerabend, 1978; Mitroff, 1974. Mitroff's evidence for effective "counternormal" behavior is a good deal more compelling than Feyerabend's.

about what counts as a "good" scientific theory, it seems utterly mysterious that those same scientists should ever (let alone often) reach a point where they eventually agree about which paradigm is acceptable. But without such agreement, the onset of normal science, whose existence Kuhn went to such lengths to document, becomes utterly unintelligible. Without an account of consensus formation, we are missing a crucial link between the two central ingredients in Kuhn's picture: his theory of disagreement (incommensurability) and his theory of consensus maintenance (normal science). Kuhn has often been faulted for failing to explain the transition from "normal" science to "crisis" science (i.e., from consensus to dissensus), because he never explained why recalcitrant but unthreatening puzzles should suddenly come to be regarded as paradigm-threatening anomalies. There is some justice in this criticism, but it misidentifies the core flaw in Kuhn's approach: that he has no plausible resources for explaining the far more striking transition from crisis to normal science. Once disagreement emerges in a scientific community, it is almost impossible to see how Kuhn can put the rabbit back into the box. When one considers how central the notion of consensus is to Kuhn's picture of science (after all, a paradigm is just what there is supposed to be consensus about, and normal science is just the sort of science that ensues when consensus reigns), it seems extraordinary that he offers no detailed account of the mechanisms of consensus formation. Worse that that, Kuhn's analysis has several features built into it which seem to foreclose any possibility of accounting for the emergence of consensus. Consider the fact that, in Kuhn's view, every paradigm is virtually self-authenticating: "each paradigm will be shown to satisfy more or less the criteria that it dictates for itself and to fall short of those dictated by its opponents."[21] If paradigms do indeed have this self-reinforcing character, then it is incomprehensible how the advocates of one paradigm might ever find reasons that would lead them to change their paradigmatic allegiances. Because Kuhn cannot explain how the advocates of rival paradigms might ever come to agree about which paradigm is better, he is in the hopeless position of requiring us to accept the existence of two radically distinct species of scientific life ("normal" and "revolutionary" science) without giving us any clues as to the dynamic process of metamorphosis, by which consensus emerges out of dissensus. Periods

21. Kuhn, 1962, pp. 108-109.

of revolutionary and normal science may each make a kind of sense in its own right, but Kuhn has no convincing story to tell about how science moves from one state to the other. Nor is it difficult to see why Kuhn lacks a theory of consensus formation: his account of dissensus requires such deep-rooted divergences and incommensurabilities between scientists that there remains no common foundation upon which to shape agreement anew.

It would be misleading to give the impression that Kuhn has nothing to say about the emergence of consensus; he does address the issue on occasion. Indeed, he goes so far as to say that what is virtually "unique" to science is that consensus emerges so convincingly out of dissensus.[22] Additionally, he devotes an entire chapter of *Structure* to answering what is essentially the question of consensus formation: "What causes the group [i.e., a scientific community] to abandon one tradition of normal research in favor of another?"[23] But what he does have to say is, when taken collectively, inconsistent, and, when taken singly, unconvincing. Sometimes, for instance, Kuhn will explain the transition from consensus in favor of one paradigm to consensus for a rival by invoking purely external considerations. We have to wait, he says, for the older generation to die off before the new paradigm establishes hegemony (the so-called Planck principle).[24] But, even if true, this provides no answer to the central question; for it fails to explain (if it be so) why the *younger* scientists are able to agree that one particular rival to the orthodoxy is preferable to others. After all, transitional periods of crisis are, for Kuhn, typified by the existence of a multitude of new paradigms, each vying for the allegiance of the relevant scientific practitioners. Even if we assume (with Kuhn) that younger scientists are more open to novelty than their elders, we still have no explanation for the fact that the young Turks are so often able to agree about which dark horse to back. If Kuhn is right about incommensurability of beliefs and incompatibility of standards, young advocates of

22. Kuhn (ibid., p. 17) writes: "What is surprizing, and perhaps also unique in its degree to the fields we call science, is that such initial divergences should ever largely disappear."

23. Ibid., pp. 143 ff.

24. The Planck principle is summed up in Max Planck's famous quip (1949, pp. 33-34): "a new scientific truth does not triumph by convincing its opponents and making them see the light, but rather because its opponents eventually die and a new generation grows up that is familiar with it." For an excellent critique of the implications of Kuhn's version of the Planck principle, see Hull, 1978.

rival paradigms should have all the same difficulties their elders do in reaching agreement about the respective merits of competing paradigms. Identical objections apply to Kuhn's suggestion that hegemony and normal science reassert themselves once the advocates of a particular paradigm get control of the major journals and the prestige appointments in a discipline. Even if true, such a reduction of scientific decision making to *Realpolitik* leaves unexplained the processes whereby the scientific elite in science comes to rally around a single new paradigm.

On other occasions, sounding rather more traditional, Kuhn says that consensus eventually congeals around a new paradigm because it can be seen to be objectively better than its predecessor by such criteria as its degree of empirical support, its demonstrated fertility, and its perceived problem-solving ability.[25] But if it is possible to compare theories along these vectors so as to get all or most scientists to agree about them, then it is unclear what all of Kuhn's earlier fuss about incommensurability and the absence of shared standards amounted to. He cannot have it both ways. Either there are shared and unambiguous standards which can be invoked by the proponents of rival paradigms for deciding the issue between them (in which case Kuhn's talk about incommensurability and the nonspecificity of shared cognitive values comes to naught, thus undermining his explanation of dissensus), or else there are no such standards (in which case Kuhn's account of disagreement escapes unscathed but only at the apparent expense of his being unable to explain consensus formation).

Kuhn is scarcely unique among contemporary philosophers and sociologists of science in propounding an account of disagreement which leaves little or no scope for explaining agreement. Imre Lakatos and Paul Feyerabend, for instance, are in the same plight, if for rather different reasons. Lakatos went to great lengths to stress the role of various conventions in theory assessment. For him, the decision to treat a prima facie falsifying instance as a genuine refutation was a matter of "convention." Mindful of the Duhemian ambiguities of falsification, Lakatos argued that rational scientists could completely ignore apparent refutations for their research programs. If they do, it becomes entirely conceivable that rival theorists might conduct a controversy for years, even decades, without the disagreement issuing in any firm

25. For this side of Kuhn's work, see especially the last chapters of Kuhn, 1962.

consensus. But what Lakatos always left opaque was how a community of scientists might reasonably come to the conclusion that one research program was genuinely superior to another, thereby reestablishing consensus. On Lakatos's account, as on Kuhn's, it appears reasonable to hang onto a theory—no matter what empirical anomalies confront it—more or less indefinitely. But to say as much is, in effect, to say that there are no rational mechanisms whereby consensus about the preferability of one line of research over another can be established. Since that sort of consensus is commonplace in the sciences, Lakatos's approach leaves us with no explanation of the fact that scientists come, often quite rapidly, to regard most scientific controversies as definitively resolved.

If Lakatos was an anarchist in spite of himself, Feyerabend set out quite deliberately to elaborate a theory of knowledge which would favor rampant theoretical pluralism. In Feyerabend's view of the matter, it is undesirable that scientists should ever reach consensus about anything. His ideal of science is the sort of endless questioning of fundamentals which one associates with pre-Socratic natural philosophy: nothing is taken as given, everything can reasonably be denied or affirmed. Like Kuhn, Feyerabend believes in the radical incommensurability of theories. Far more than Kuhn, he denies that there are any methodological principles or norms which it is reasonable to insist that scientists follow in assessing theories ("anything goes"). Feyerabend does not deny that scientists sometimes do agree about which theories are good and which are bad, but he deplores that state of affairs as unreasonable. If scientists only appreciated the finer points of epistemology, he seems to say, they would see that no theories should ever be regarded as having displaced or discredited their rivals and predecessors.

Sociologists, too, have been quick to see that the existence of widespread controversy in science fits ill with older models of science in their field. Michael Mulkay seems to speak for many of the new-wave theorists in regarding the phenomenon of scientific disagreement as a refutation of older approaches: "If, for example, the Mertonian norms are effectively institutionalized in science, it becomes difficult to account for the frequency of intellectual resistance [which] is recurrent in science and is, indeed, an inescapable feature of the growth of scientific knowledge."[26]

26. Mulkay, 1977, p. 106.

A preoccupation with scientific disagreement has lately shown up with increasing frequency in the research of several sociologists of science, including Collins, Pickering, and Pinch. Harry Collins, for instance, has devoted much effort to studying some recent controversies in theoretical physics. In each of the cases Collins examined, he found that ingenious scientists can concoct a way to circumvent arguments and evidence against their pet theories. In effect, Collins's claim is that the experimental evidence is always so ambiguous that virtually any theory can be maintained in the face of any evidence. As he puts it, "the natural world in no way constrains what is believed to be."[27] Or, "the natural world has a small or non-existent role in the construction of scientific knowledge."[28] Since, in Collins's view, the features of the world (as we come to learn about them from experiment and observation) do virtually nothing to restrain our beliefs about the world, Collins has a ready explanation for the prolongation of scientific disagreement. But, as with Lakatos, Feyerabend, and Kuhn, that explanatory virtue quickly becomes a liability because, having severed all significant causal links between the world and our beliefs about it, Collins cannot bring the world back into the picture as a factor driving scientists to eventual consensus. Although Collins says he is interested in the mechanisms of consensus formation in science (he asserts it is important to describe the "mechanisms which *limit* interpretative flexibility and thus allow controversies to come to an end"),[29] I predict he will find that, having written off the world as a constraint on our beliefs, he lacks the most relevant explanatory resources for tackling that problem. Like the others, Collins seems to be in the awkward position of having so robustly explained how scientists can disagree that it becomes nothing short of miraculous that scientists are frequently able to reach a broad agreement about the "facts" of the world and about which theories are the most promising or plausible for explaining those facts.

In this brief thumbnail sketch of some currents in contemporary philosophy and sociology of science, I have not attempted to establish that any of the new-wave approaches are false or that their flaws are irremediable. But what does seem clear is that the newly forming orthodoxy in philosophy and sociology of science is confronted by challenges

27. Collins, 1981*a*, p. 54.
28. Collins, 1981*b*, p. 3.
29. Ibid., p. 4.

every bit as daunting as those that proved to be the undoing of empiricist methodology and Mertonian sociology. More specifically, many recent theorists, while labeling classical philosophy and sociology as impoverished, have ignored the central issues with which their predecessors were grappling. We can scarcely claim to have moved significantly beyond the work of the 1940s and 1950s unless we can make some sense of the striking facts that scholars of that generation rightly regarded as basic features of science. We either have to deny with Feyerabend that rational scientists could ever exhibit widespread agreement (and that seems to run counter to the record), or else we have to find some account of dissensus which is not so robust that it precludes the very possibility of frequent and widespread agreement. Until we manage to account for a Janus-faced science, we cannot seriously claim to have understood what we are about.

This book is an attempt to move us some steps forward in that direction. In succeeding chapters I focus chiefly on describing the various levels at which scientific disagreement can occur. In each instance we will be exploring how far one can expect disagreements to be amenable to rational analysis and rational closure. As we shall come to see, the full-blown Leibnizian ideal cannot be plausibly resurrected, for there remain many scientific controversies that cannot be rationally terminated, even with the best will in the world. On the other hand, we will discover a very large range of cases where there is appropriate analytic machinery for understanding how many scientific controversies can be brought to a reasonably definitive resolution.

Chapter Two

THE HIERARCHICAL STRUCTURE OF SCIENTIFIC DEBATES

In any community as diverse as the scientific one, and especially in one with such a deeply entrenched tradition of challenges to authority, where successful breaks with tradition are handsomely rewarded, consensus is not born but made. Because agreement typically emerges out of prior disagreement, it is useful to cast the puzzle of consensus formation in this form: How is it that a very high proportion of scientists, who previously had different (and often mutually incompatible) views about a particular subject, can eventually come to hold substantially identical views about that subject? Put this way, the problem of consensus formation is a problem about the dynamics of convergent belief change.

The best-known contemporary solution to the problem of consensus formation in science involves postulating what I call the hierarchical model of justification, although it is perhaps more commonly known as the theory of instrumental rationality. Proponents of this model[1] typically envisage three interrelated levels at which, and by means of which, scientific consensus is forged. At the lowest level of this hierarchy are disputes about matters of fact. By the phrase "matters of fact" I mean to refer not only to assertions about directly observable events but to all manner of claims about what there is in the world, including claims about theoretical or unobservable entities. For obvi-

---

1. Among the influential philosophical advocates of the hierarchical model are Karl Popper, C. G. Hempel, and Hans Reichenbach.

ous reasons, I call debates of this sort "factual disagreements," and agreement at this level, "factual consensus." According to the standard account, scientists resolve factual disagreements and thus forge factual consensus by moving one step up the hierarchy to the level of shared methodological rules. The rules may be mechanical algorithms for generating factual statements. But, much more typically, the rules will simply be constraints or injunctions concerning the attributes we should seek (e.g., independent testability) or avoid (e.g., ad hocness) in our theories. As normally understood, such rules, which are basically principles of empirical support and of comparative theory assessment, provide directives for ascertaining, at least in a qualitative sense, how much support (i.e., confirmation or disconfirmation) the available evidence provides for the theories under evaluation. If two scientists disagree about whether one rival factual claim or another is more worthy of belief, they have (in this view) but to compare the weights of support enjoyed by their respective claims in order to terminate their disagreement.

According to this model, decisions between competing theories may be likened to the way in which our courts settle, or are supposed to settle, civil contests: relevant evidence is presented; the court agrees to shape its verdict according to well-established jurisprudential rules of evidence; an impartial verdict is "guaranteed" because the issue is settled in light of the rules rather than of personalities; and, finally, all the parties to the case agree to abide by the verdict. In the same way, the hierarchical model requires that scientists submit their factual disputes to a kind of invisible "science court" (in this case, the practitioners of one or another scientific specialty). The "scientific jury" is expected to make its choice according to rules of evidential support agreed to by all scientists working in that specialty. Such prior agreement is thought to guarantee that the "verdict" will be both impartial and acceptable to all parties. At first glance, this approach has much going for it. It can explain not only why scientific disagreements often issue in consensus, but also the rapidity with which they do so. (And as pointed out in chapter 1, the really remarkable thing about many scientific controversies is how quickly they are brought to a definitive resolution.)

The thesis that factual disagreements can be resolved by invoking the relevant rules of evidence is, of course, just a modern exemplification of what I have earlier called the "Leibnizian ideal." But whereas that ideal in its original form imagined that all factual disagreements could be terminated by invoking the relevant rules, latter-day proponents of methodological rules tend to be more modest. They continue to believe that some disagreements can be immediately resolved by utilizing the available evidence (and the shared rules). Failing that, however, they go on to say that the rules are often sufficiently specific to indicate procedures for the collection of such additional evidence as will bring the issue to a definitive resolution. The rules themselves vary from the highly general ("formulate testable and simple hypotheses") to those of intermediate generality ("prefer the results of double-blind to single-blind experiments"), to those specific to a particular discipline or even subdiscipline ("make sure to calibrate instrument x against standard y"). To the extent that these procedural or methodological rules are accepted by all parties to the dispute, and insofar as they are sufficiently specific to determine a choice between the available rivals, they should indeed suffice for the mediation of factual controversies. And a staggeringly large proportion of factual disputes have evidently been ended simply by observing the relevant methodological procedures.

Sometimes, however, scientists disagree about the appropriate rules of evidence or procedure, or about how those rules are to be applied to the case at hand.[2] In such circumstances, the rules can no longer be treated as an unproblematic instrument for resolving factual disagreement. When this happens, it becomes clear that a particular factual disagreement betokens a deeper methodological disagreement. In the standard hierarchical view, such methodological controversies are to be resolved by moving one step up the hierarchy, that is, by reference to the shared aims or goals of science. This suggestion is a natural one

---

2. The fact that scientists sometimes subscribe to different methodological principles stands as an important anomaly to Andrew Lugg's otherwise very stimulating account (1978) of the causes of scientific disagreement. Lugg's general thesis is that disagreements about substantive scientific matters may arise because scientists have, in effect, differential degrees of access to the data base potentially relevant to the assessment of any theory. Thus, practitioners working in one subspecialty will usually have a different perspective on the degree of support enjoyed by competing theories from that employed by the corresponding specialists in another branch of the science. Lugg is surely right in deeming difference as one source of disagreement. But he is wrong in suggesting that a community of "ideal" observers, each of whom had access to all the relevant available evidence, would be bound to produce a consensual science. For to say as much is to ignore the real differences of methodological orientation which scientists, even when confronted by the same evidence, often exhibit.

to make, for a little reflection makes clear that methodological rules possess what force they have because they are believed to be instruments or means for achieving the aims of science. More generally, both in science and elsewhere, we adopt the procedural and evaluative rules we do because we hold them to be optimal techniques for realizing our cognitive goals or utilities. Hence, when two scientists find themselves espousing different and conflicting methodological rules (and assuming, as the standard account does, that they have the same basic aims), they can in principle terminate their disagreement at the methodological level by determining which of the rival rules conduce(s) most effectively to achieving the collective goals of science. I call this third stage, where basic cognitive aims are involved, the axiological level.

We can therefore sum up the prevailing philosophical view on scientific disagreements succinctly: disagreements about factual matters are to be resolved at the methodological level; methodological differences are to be ironed out at the axiological level.[3] Axiological differences are thought to be either nonexistent (on the grounds that scientists are presumed to share the same goals) or else, should they exist, irresolvable (see fig. 1). In the rest of this chapter I explore some of the strengths of, and objections to, this pervasive model of consensus formation.

FACTUAL CONSENSUS FORMATION

One apparent weakness of the hierarchical view lies in its central assumption that methodological rules will, at least in principle, always pick out one factual claim, to the exclusion of all its possible rivals, as uniquely supported by those rules. Yet it is notorious that methodological rules usually underdetermine a choice among factual claims in the sense that, although the rules plus the available evidence will exclude many factual claims or hypotheses, a plethora of possible hypotheses

3. There is an excellent formulation of the hierarchical view of the relation between methods and aims in Gutting, 1973. Squarely in the hierarchical tradition, Gutting stresses that methodological disputes can often be resolved by looking to the "founding intentions" or the aims of the members of a scientific community. This is to ignore (a) that those intentions themselves do not remain constant through time and, more important, (b) that scientists are often unable to agree on what the founding intentions of a discipline are. In such circumstances, Gutting, like every other advocate of the hierarchical view, proposes no remedies for mediating disagreement (see esp. Gutting, 1973, pp. 277 ff.).

Level of Disagreement	*Level of Resolution*
Factual	Methodological
Methodological	Axiological
Axiological	None

Fig. 1. The Simple Hierarchical Model of Rational Consensus Formation

often remains methodologically admissible. Among the admissible hypotheses may be some that are evidentially equivalent, in that no conceivable evidence could ever discriminate among them. It is often said, for instance, that certain versions of wave and matrix mechanics are observationally equivalent. In such circumstance, it is clear that no observations could ever decisively choose between them. In other cases the admissible hypotheses will be evidentially distinct (in the sense that there is conceivable evidence that would differentially support them) but such that the existing evidence and the prevailing rules do not provide grounds for a preference. Since the set of factual claims supported by certain methodological rules can be shown always to include several contraries of one another,[4] it is often charged that the underdetermination of theory by the relevant rules and evidence makes a mockery of the hierarchical model of consensus formation (at least when that model is applied to the adjudication of disagreements about theories). But this commonplace criticism generally misses the point. What we usually want to explain in any particular instance of consensus formation is not how scientists were able to agree to accept a certain hypothesis rather than every other possible hypothesis. If that were our explanatory puzzle, then methodological underdetermination would indeed preclude an answer. Equally, if the partisans of rival scientific theories were looking to find out if one of their theories was better supported than all possible rivals, then this sort of underdetermination would be debilitating. But this is to misstate the problem in both cases. What scientists are trying to decide (and here our earlier judicial analogy is especially apt) is not whether their theories will last for all time, or whether they will always stack up favorably against all conceivable rivals; rather they are trying to decide which of the theories presently contending in the scientific marketplace is best supported by the evidence. Scientists, in the view I am advocating, should be seen, not as looking for simply the best theory, but rather for the best theory they

---

4. For a more detailed treatment of underdetermination, see chap. 4 below.

can find. I am suggesting that a more constructive, and a more realistic, way of formulating the problem of consensus formation is this: Given that some scientists once believed one theory and that others once accepted a rival to it, why do they all now accept the latter?[5] In other words, we are usually seeking to understand why a particular preference was made consensually to endorse one from among a finite (and usually quite narrow) range of articulated rival theories. To make it more concrete, we want to find answers to such questions as these: Why did geologists, who once heaped such scorn on the theory of continental drift, eventually come to accept plate tectonics? Why did physicists, who once were advocates of the corpuscular theory of light, eventually come to believe that the undular theory was a better bet?

Once we put the problem of consensus formation in this comparative mode, we take much of the sting out of the argument from underdetermination. For in many instances the shared rules and the existing evidence neatly partition the extant theories under active consideration into two sets, those that, according to the rules, are supported by the evidence and those that are not. In the event that both parties to a controversy draw their theories from among the elements of the former set, then the methodological rules will clearly be insufficient to mandate a preference and the participants will simply have to agree to disagree — pending the accumulation of further evidence. Instances of such (temporary) underdetermination arise fairly often, and they are, of course, the most interesting ones for historians and sociologists of science to examine. But the appeal of such long-term standoffs ought not blind us to the fact that they are arguably a tiny minority of cases. Most of the time all the parties to the dispute will agree that there comes a point where the rules unambiguously warrant a preference among the extant competing theories.

One might wonder how I can say that rules can simultaneously underdetermine belief and determine a preference. This distinction is elementary, but it needs to be attended to carefully, for numerous authors have been confused by it. Essentially, a rule (or a set of rules) partitions prospective beliefs into two classes, the permissible and the impermissible. A belief is permissible precisely when, among the various alternatives to it under active consideration, none has a higher

---

5. I have formulated the problem for a choice between two rival theories; it could readily be generalized to apply to a larger number.

degree of empirical support than it does.[6] If we define permissible beliefs in this way, we see that several rival claims about a certain matter of fact may all be permissible in the face of a certain body of evidence. That is, they may all be equally well supported. However, and here is the contrast with strict underdetermination, there can be circumstances in which one rival alone among those under active consideration is significantly better supported by the evidence than the others. In such cases that rival alone is permissible; its acceptance, rather than the acceptance of any of its known rivals, is unambiguously dictated by the germane rules and evidence.

Of course, the preferred rival may still be underdetermined in the strict sense of the term, since there may be conceivable, but thus far unconceived, rival theories that would be as well supported as our permissible choice. The crucial point here is that even when a rule underdetermines choice in the abstract, that same rule may still unambiguously dictate a comparative preference among extant alternatives. It will do so specifically when we are confronted with a choice between (in the simplest case) two candidate theories, one of which is (methodologically) permissible and the other not.

For instance, the rules and evidence of biology, although they do not establish the unique correctness of evolutionary theory, do exclude numerous creationist hypotheses—for example, the claim that the earth is between 10,000 and 20,000 years old—from the permissible realm and thus provide a warrant for a rational preference for evolutionary over creationist biology. If we once grant that theory appraisal is a comparative matter, that the scientist is generally making comparative judgments of adequacy among available rivals rather than absolute judgments about the best possible theory, then it becomes clear that comparative preferences may be warranted even when the selection of the best possible theory is beyond our justificatory resources.

I review this familiar terrain because several recent writers[7] have been apt to ignore the difference between (what I am here calling)

---

6. Tough-minded readers may want to work with a more demanding sense of permissible belief, according to which a belief is regarded as warranted only if it enjoys stronger support from the rules than all its extant rivals. (Otherwise, we might find ourselves in a situation where contrary beliefs were all permissible.) I would myself resist the stronger characterization of "permissible," but the argument I develop here in the text will work, whichever formulation of permissible one inclines to.

7. Including Quine, Hesse, and Bloor.

choices and preferences. Specifically, they appear to have argued that, since theory choice is underdetermined by methodological rules, it follows that no rational preference is possible among rival theories, which entails, in turn, that every theory is as well supported as any other, and that every party to a scientific debate is thus as rational as every other. Our discussion should have made clear that the thesis of underdetermination, in its viable forms, provides no justification for the view that all theories are equally well confirmed or equally rational in light of a given body of empirical information. The implications of this point might be discussed at greater length if our concern were chiefly with the logic and methodology of theory evaluation. But it is sufficient for our purposes here to note that the slide from underdetermination to what we might call cognitive egalitarianism (i.e., the thesis that all beliefs are epistemically or evidentially equal in terms of their support) must be resisted, for it confusedly takes the fact that our rules fail to pick out a unique theory that satisfies them as a warrant for asserting the inability of the rules to make any discriminations whatever with respect to which theories are or are not in compliance with them.

In its extreme form, such egalitarianism amounts to a radical version of epistemic relativism, one formulation of which can be found in the thesis of the sociologist Harry Collins that, because our beliefs are not uniquely determined by the evidence, our beliefs can reasonably be presumed to be independent of the evidence for them! In a less extreme and more carefully articulated form, one sees the same sort of argument in Thomas Kuhn's recent work (especially in *The Essential Tension*) on the role of rules and values in science. Like Wittgenstein before him, Kuhn makes much of the fact that there are no algorithms for scientific choice; that is, we have no agreed-upon rules that would uniquely pick out the best possible theory in light of a given body of evidence and background assumptions. What rules we do have, Kuhn seems to think, are invariably so ambiguous that they are of little practical use in making specific theory choices. Kuhn is not dismissive of rules; nor, like certain skeptical sociologists, does he regard them as so many post hoc rationalizations. To the contrary, Kuhn insists that methodological rules play both a causal and a justificatory role in scientific belief. But because Kuhn also believes that the rules of appraisal are highly ambiguous and fluid (he likens them to such homespun and largely uninformative maxims as "look before you leap"), he inclines to assign them a minimal role. He says, for instance, that because we have no rules that would unambiguously pick out a single theory to the exclusion of all other possible theories about the relevant domain, it is inevitable that the choice between any two theories could always go one way or the other, given any set of values or norms about what we expect our theories to achieve. Kuhn is not denying that rules play a role in the choice of scientific theories, but he is insisting that their intrinsic ambiguity precludes the possibility of decisive preferences ever being justified on the basis of shared methodological rules. Kuhn grants that "such canons [his examples are accuracy, simplicity, generality, etc.] do exist and should be discoverable," but he goes on to insist that "they are not by themselves sufficient to determine the decisions of individual scientists."[8] If all that Kuhn is saying here is that general rules and values underdetermine choice (in the strict sense defined above), one might not quarrel with his claim; but, as his subsequent discussion makes clear, he is asserting — to use my earlier language — that preferences are underdetermined as well. He puts it this way: "every individual choice between competing theories depends on a mixture of objective and subjective factors, of shared and individual criteria."[9] Kuhn thinks that this state of affairs must be so because, according to his analysis, the "objective" criteria shared by scientists cannot justify one preference to the exclusion of another. Since, as Kuhn knows perfectly well, scientists do in fact voice theory preferences, he takes this as evidence that they must be working with various individual and idiosyncratic criteria that go well beyond the shared ones. Without the latter, he seems to say, how could scientists ever have preferences? But neither Kuhn nor anyone else has shown, either in fact or in principle, that such rules and evaluative criteria as are shared among scientists are generally or invariably insufficient to indicate unambiguous grounds for preference of certain theories over others.

Indeed, using some of Kuhn's own criteria, we can show precisely how a rationally based preference can arise. Suppose that a scientist is confronted with a choice between specific versions of Aristotle's physics and Newton's physics. Suppose moreover that the scientist is committed to observational accuracy as a primary value. Even granting with Kuhn that "accuracy" is usually not precisely defined, and even

8. Kuhn, 1977, pp. 324-325.
9. Ibid., p. 325.

though different scientists may interpret accuracy in subtly different ways, I submit that it was incontestable by the late seventeenth century that Newton's theory was empirically more accurate than Aristotle's. Indeed, even Newton's most outspoken critics conceded that his theory was empirically more accurate than all its ancient predecessors. Similarly, if it comes to a choice between Kepler's laws and Newton's planetary astronomy—and it does come to such a choice since the two are formally incompatible—and if our primary standard is, say, scope or generality of application (another of the cognitive values cited by Kuhn), then our preference is once again dictated by our values. At best, Kepler's laws apply only to large planetary masses; Newton's theory applies to all masses whatsoever. Under such circumstances the rule, "prefer theories of greater generality," gives unequivocal advice. There will, of course, be times when the shared criteria are too ambiguous to yield a definitive preference; such cases have tended to preoccupy Kuhn in his analysis of scientific change. But when he generalizes from such arguably idiosyncratic cases to make claims about "every individual choice between competing theories" being immune to resolution by the shared rules, and when he goes on to suggest that no one has ever denied that his account is "simply descriptive of what goes on in the sciences at times of theory choice,"[10] it is necessary to set the record straight by pointing out that neither Kuhn nor anyone else has shown that most (let alone all) theory choice situations exhibit the impotence of "shared criteria" to determine a preference.

In other words, although Kuhn is surely right to stress that we have no perfectly general logic of confirmation or comprehensive theory of evidence, just as he is right to say that many rules are ambiguous, he is wrong to see these facts as sustaining the claim that the application of shared scientific rules or values to a specific choice situation will always be (or always has been) ambiguous or unavailing. There are some situations where it is unavailing; we have already discussed some of these under the general head of "underdetermination." But Kuhn has neither shown, nor even made plausible, the claim that the rules, evaluative criteria, and values to which scientists subscribe are so ambiguous in application that virtually any theory can be shown to satisfy them. And we must constantly bear in mind the point, already made, that even when theories are underdetermined by a set of rules, there will

10. Ibid., p. 325.

typically be many theories ruled out by the operant rules; and if one party to a scientific debate happens to be pushing for a theory that can be shown to violate those rules, then the rules will eliminate that theory from contention.

It follows from this analysis that the hierarchical model is not (as many of its critics claim) rendered toothless by the argument from underdetermination. To the contrary, it seems entirely reasonable to say that many disputes about matters of fact have been terminated by invoking shared procedural rules. But it is important to realize what "hedges" are built into this reformulation of the hierarchical view. Not all factual disagreements can be resolved in this Leibnizian fashion because two or more extant rivals may be equally well supported by the existing rules and evidence. Similarly, it may happen (a case that I will explore shortly) that scientists differ about which evidential rules should be applied to the case at hand. The fact that this version of the hierarchical model leads us to expect consensus only in some instances will satisfy neither the archrationalist advocates of the Leibnizian ideal (who want an in-principle, instant termination for every factual disagreement) nor the proponents of radical underdetermination (who believe in the potential prolongation of every disagreement indefinitely). But the strength of this version of the hierarchical model is that it can (unlike the underdeterminationists) specify circumstances in which we would expect a factual disagreement to dissolve into consensus and it can (unlike the Leibnizian idealists) also specify a broad range of circumstances in which we would expect factual dissensus to endure.

METHODOLOGICAL CONSENSUS FORMATION

Thus far we have been uncritically accepting one central feature of the Leibnizian picture, even while rejecting others, for we have been discussing situations in which a group of scientists shares a set of cognitive aims and methodological rules, but disagree about certain factual matters. It sometimes happens that disagreements go deeper than this. We occasionally see scientists unable to agree even about the appropriate methodological and procedural rules to bring to bear on the choice of hypotheses or theories. One scientist, for instance, may believe (with Popper) that a theory must make surprising, even startling, predictions, which turn out to be correct, before it is reasonable to accept it.

Another may be willing to accept a hypothesis so long as it explains a broad range of phenomena, even if it has not made startling predictions. A third may say (with Nagel) that no theory is worth its salt until it has been tested against a wide variety of different kinds of supporting instances. A fourth may believe that a very large number of confirmations is probatively significant, regardless of the variety they exhibit. A fifth may demand that there be some direct and independent evidence for the existence of the entities postulated by a hypothesis before it can reasonably be accepted. All these familiar methodological principles of theory acceptance are at odds with one another, and each has found prominent advocates in recent science and philosophy.

What are we to say when scientists disagree about the rules of the scientific game? Is there any hope, apart from artificially imposing closure from outside the system, that scientists can reasonably resolve their methodological differences? Or are they caught up in a nasty normative incommensurability which defies rational solution? The answer to that question depends, according to the hierarchical model, on our ability to resolve such methodological controversies by moving one step up the cognitive ladder of justification.

To see how the hierarchy comes into it, we have to remind ourselves of the function of, and thus of the rationale for, rules in general. We generally agree to govern an activity (whether it is science, chess, or parliamentary debate) by a particular set of rules when we think that those rules will enable us to achieve the ends or goals that define the telos of the activity. Scientists presumably have the methodological rules they do because they suppose that following the rules in question will bring about, or at least bring them closer to, the realization of their cognitive or doxastic aims. So conceived, methodological rules are nothing but putative instrumentalities for the realization of one's cognitive ends; in a word, the rules of science are designed simply as means to cognitive ends or tools for performing a task. To think about rules in this way immediately suggests an answer to our question about how to resolve disputes about rules and, in the process, offers a way out of the incommensurability that apparently ensues when people cannot agree to play the game by the same rules. It should now be clear that if two scientists disagree about the appropriate rules but agree about some "higher" cognitive values or ends, then we can possibly resolve the disagreement about rules by ascertaining which set of rules is most likely to realize the common cognitive aims. Once we know the answer to that question, we will know what the appropriate methodological rule(s) should be, and we will have a resolution of the methodological disagreement, at least insofar as it was rationally founded in the shared axiology.

But as plausible as this answer is in general terms (and I believe that it is on the right track), it makes things seem a good deal tidier than they really are and it leaves several important issues unaddressed. For instance, it presupposes that a given set of cognitive aims or goals is uniquely associated with a certain set of methodological rules, that is, that a particular set of rules can be shown to be the only optimal means for achieving the values in question. It is generally difficult, and in certain cases patently impossible, to exhibit that a particular set of rules is the best possible way for realizing a certain set of values. More modestly, but just as usefully, we may be able to show that following a particular set of rules will indeed realize a certain epistemic value, although it may be quite another matter to show that these rules are the best or the only means for achieving the values we desire. And if we cannot demonstrate the latter, then we cannot argue for the blanket superiority of those rules over all their conceivable rivals for realizing the values in question. In short — and this is crucial — cognitive aims typically underdetermine methodological rules in precisely the same way that methodological rules characteristically underdetermine factual choices. The classic philosopher's quest to show that certain procedures of inquiry are the only route to a desired epistemic end is a largely misguided one, because we cannot usually enumerate, let alone examine, all the possible ways of achieving a certain goal. And without such an examination we usually have no warrant for asserting that one set of methods is superior to all the others. To make the point less abstractly, one can observe that with respect to such familiar cognitive goals as truth, coherence, simplicity, and predictive fertility, scholars have not managed to show that there is any set of rules of empirical investigation which uniquely conduces to their realization. In sum, rules, like theories, are underdetermined by the relevant constraints.

And a good thing they are too. For if there was only one set of rules for realizing any specific set of cognitive aims, we should have to conclude that it was irrational for scientists sharing the same ends or values ever to disagree about the appropriate rules for implementing those values. Yet such disputes are chronic in the history of science and philosophy. Consider, for instance, the 150-year-long (and still ongoing) controversy about the so-called rule of predesignation.[11] This rule specifies that a hypothesis is tested only by the new predictions drawn from it, not by its ability post hoc to explain what was already known. A host of prominent thinkers have been arrayed on each side of this issue (Whewell, Peirce, and Popper for predesignation; Mill and Keynes, among others, against it). All parties to the controversy would, I believe, subscribe to substantially the same cognitive aims. They seek theories that are true, general, simple, and explanatory. Yet no one has been able to show whether the rule of predesignation is the best, or even an appropriate, means for reaching those ends. That failure is entirely typical. There is almost no cognitive value and associated methodological rule which have been shown to stand in this one-to-one relation to each other. So far as we know, there may be equally viable methods for achieving all the cognitive goals usually associated with science. It is for just this reason, incidentally, that the much sought-after "scientific method" may be a will-o'-the-wisp. To seek the rules of *the* scientific method is to presuppose that there is only one legitimate means to the achievement of the shared cognitive aims of science. Because there may well be a variety of methodological rules which conduce equally well to achieving our cognitive values, it follows that the coexistence of nonidentical methods of inquiry may well be a permanent feature of scientific life.[12]

But, the skeptic may ask, if we can never justify a methodological rule by showing it to be the only or the optimal means for achieving a certain cognitive value, how can we—as I have claimed—use the aims and values of science as a tool for resolving disputes about methodological rules? Shared goals can often mediate controversies about rules precisely because they impose constraints on the class of permissible rules. We can sometimes show, for instance, that certain rules are nonconducive, even counterconducive, to achieving certain values. If, for example, one of our cognitive values is generality and breadth of scope in our theories, then it is quite clear that any appraisal rule that

11. I discuss the early history of the rule of predesignation in Laudan, 1981.

12. A second, probably insuperable, obstacle to the quest for *the* scientific method is the absence of a full consensus among scientists about what the cognitive goals of science should be. Without that agreement we should scarcely be surprised if some dissensus about methods persists. (But it should be stressed, as noted below, pp. 43 ff., that a lack of consensus about cognitive aims does not necessarily entail the existence of any dissensus about the appropriate methods.)

insists that we should accept only highly probably theories is unsatisfactory. Precisely because one can (following Popper) demonstrate an incompatibility between high probability and broad explanatory scope, we can quickly exclude a rule urging maximally high probabilities from the methodological repertoire of anyone whose primary cognitive aims include generality. Hence, one role of aims in resolving methodological disagreements is to eliminate certain methodological rules, by virtue of their irreconcilability with those aims.

Besides this exclusionary function, aims can sometimes play a positive role, as, for example, when we can show that certain methodological rules promote certain cognitive values. For, although we generally cannot show that a particular rule is the best of all possible rules for realizing a certain end, we often can show both (1) that it is one way of realizing a particular end, and (2) that it is better than all its rivals that are under active consideration. And this result will often be sufficient to resolve a particular disagreement about methodological rules. If, for instance, we can show that one particular rule is a better way to achieve given cognitive ends than a rival rule is, and if the controversy is specifically between advocates of those two rules (who, moreover, have a shared set of cognitive aims), then we are in a clear position to move the controversy rationally to closure.

But although the invocation of shared goals may sometimes make methodological consensus possible, it is crucial to stress that this is not a cure-all for all manner of methodological disagreements. It may happen, for instance, that both parties to the controversy are advocating methodological rules that are, so far as we can see, equally effective means to achieving the cognitive values in question. Even more seriously (and more commonly), we may find ourselves in a situation where we endorse a broad range of cognitive aims or values simultaneously (say, simplicity, coherence, and empirical accuracy). A methodological rule may tend to promote the realization of one of these values while it thwarts the realization of another. Is the rule, under such circumstances, a good one or a bad one? The answer depends, in part, on how we respectively weight the goals we endorse. If the rule promotes those goals that are the most important to us, we may find the rule acceptable. Yet someone who subscribes to the same cognitive goals, but weights them differently, may well find the rule unacceptable. Methodological disagreements such as these show little promise of adjudication by bringing aims explicitly into play. Equally problematic is the situation where the disagreement about rules derives from an even deeper disagreement about cognitive aims (discussed in detail in chap. 3).

But before we move on to deal with the very tricky case of disagreements about basic goals, we should pause a moment to reflect on some of the implications of our account of the resolution of methodological disagreements. If the analysis sketched here is correct, we have to realize that the vertical hierarchy of facts-rules-aims has a rather more complex structure than figure 1 and our earlier discussion might suggest. Although we appraise methodological rules by asking whether they conduce to cognitive ends (suggesting movement up the justificatory hierarchy), the factors that settle the question are often drawn from a lower level in the hierarchy, specifically from the level of factual inquiry. Factual information comes to play a role in the assessment of methodological claims precisely because we are continuously learning new things about the world and about ourselves as observers of that world. Such knowledge comes to be formulated in theories concerning, among other things, the various complexities of the process of collecting evidence. To take an elementary example, we have learned that nature does not offer information to us in a random or statistically representative way. As medium-sized objects in a world replete with the very small and the very large, the entities and processes we are most likely to encounter in our everyday scrutiny of the world are highly unrepresentative of that world in many crucial respects. Once we learned that fact, it became necessary to develop elaborate sampling techniques in order to make our evidence more representative than it would have been had we simply collected whatever information casually came our way. Contrary to popular conception, the superiority of randomly collected data over nonrandomly collected data is not a discovery made by mathematics or formal logic as a feature of inquiry in all possible worlds. It is because the particular world we inhabit turns out to be so uncooperative and, as we have learned that only through hard-won experience, we find it appropriate to insist on a variety of stringent rules about sampling in order to achieve our cognitive ends.

Consider a different example. Within the past fifty years we have learned a great deal about the so-called placebo effect. In brief, many patients report an improvement upon being given any apparent medication, even if (unbeknownst to the patient) it is pharmacologically inert. Until we learned this, simple controlled experiments were regarded as sufficient tests of therapeutic efficacy. To find out if a drug worked, scientists formerly would give it to one group of patients and nothing whatever would be administered to a second (control) group with comparable symptoms. If the former reported higher rates of improvement than the latter, the test was taken as good evidence that the drug was effective. But once we learned about the placebo effect, it became clear that the testing of various new therapies (including virtually all drugs) had to be rather more complicated than we had once imagined. Specifically, scientists realized that they needed to resort to so-called single-blind tests, which make appropriate allowances for spurious reports of efficacy (i.e., reports of efficacy based largely on the patient's expectations of betterment). To make matters still more complex, once we learned further that those administering drug tests could often, if unconsciously, transmit their own therapeutic expectations to the patients they were examining, it became necessary to formulate techniques for double-blind tests of medications and other therapies.

In all these instances our views about the proper procedures for investigating the world have been significantly affected by our shifting beliefs about how the world works.[13] Factual beliefs thus shape methodological attitudes, every bit as much as our goals do. A priori reflection on our cognitive aims would not have necessitated the development of randomizing techniques or of single- and double-blind experiments. It was, rather, the realization, given what we had learned of the world, that our cognitive aims could be achieved more effectively by resorting to some such techniques which mandated their introduction and provided their justification.

What the foregoing suggests is that the methodology and epistemology of science, whose central concern is with the assessment of various rules of inquiry and validation, should be conceived, far more than they normally are, as empirical disciplines.[14] Crediting or discrediting

13. There is thus a central, but nonvicious, circularity about our evaluative procedures: we use certain methods for studying the world and those very methods may serve initially to authenticate discoveries that expose the weaknesses of those selfsame methods.

14. This suggestion should not be confused with Quine's familiar argument about "naturalized epistemology." Whereas Quine sees close affinities between psychology and epistemology, I am not committed to that particular program of reduction. My insistence, rather, is that the appraisal of proposed cognitive methods and aims requires extensive empirical research. That research will often have nothing specifically

a methodological rule requires us to ask ourselves whether the universe we inhabit is one in which our cognitive ends can in fact be furthered by following this rule rather than that. Such questions cannot be answered a priori; they are empirical matters. It follows that scientific methodology is itself an empirical discipline which cannot dispense with the very methods of inquiry whose validity it investigates. Armchair methodology is as ill-conceived as armchair chemistry or physics. There is nothing particularly new in this conception of the character of scientific methodology. More than half a century ago, John Dewey—ever eager to naturalize the a priori—repudiated that conception of methodology which saw it as "an affair . . . of fixed first principles . . . of what the Neo-scholastics called criteriology."[15] What is remarkable is that, despite massive evidence to the contrary, some philosophers of science still tend to imagine that methodology is protoscientific, that is, prior to and independent of the kind of empirical inquiry which science itself represents.

Unfortunately, many of those authors who have recently argued that epistemology and methodology should be rendered more empirical or more "naturalistic" seem to have assumed that a naturalizing of epistemology would necessarily empty it of normative force, presumably on the grounds that a truly empirical epistemology would be exclusively descriptive. Granting for a moment that there is no hard-and-fast line between normative and descriptive activities, the presumption that an empirical theory of knowledge would be void of normative claims is nonsense. Once we realize (as this chapter should make clear) that methodological norms and rules assert empirically testable relations between ends and means, it should become clear that epistemic norms, construed of course as conditional imperatives (conditional relative to a given set of aims), should form the core of a naturalistic theory of scientific knowledge. When authors like Barry Barnes suggest that "the normative concerns common among epistemologists are difficult to reconcile with an empirical orientation to science,"[16] they

---

to do with psychological phenomena. Whereas Quine evidently sees naturalized epistemology as constituting a subfield within psychology, I argue that an empirical epistemology or methodology is neither a part of, nor subordinate to, psychology. And typically, it would draw more heavily on physics and biology than on psychology.

15. Dewey, 1938.
16. Barnes, 1982, p. 63.

reveal how deeply they have misunderstood the fact that an empirical approach to epistemology requires attention to precisely those normative linkages between cognitive ends and means which constitute scientific rationality.

To conclude, we find ourselves with mixed results. There do seem to be circumstances under which both factual and methodological disagreements can be brought to a rational resolution by seeking shared assumptions at a higher level. The familiar idea that agreement about factual matters is possible only among those who already accept the same methodological rules is clearly seen to be too restrictive, for it fails to reckon with the fact that, by moving a step up the hierarchy to aims and goals, dissensus about rules may dissolve into consensus. And that consensus about rules, once in place, may be sufficient to resolve the disagreement about the contested factual matters. But we have also discovered a number of problem cases. When the shared rules fail to dictate a factual preference, when the shared goals fail to specify a methodological preference, when values are shared but not weighted equally, and when values are not fully shared, we seem to be confronted by an irresolvable disagreement — irresolvable, that is, if we stick to the limited resources of the classical hierarchical model. Most crucial of all is the situation where scientists subscribe to different goals. Such circumstances occur sufficiently often to pose a fundamental challenge to the very idea that science is a rational and progressive undertaking. But, as we shall see in chapter 3, that challenge is not always so stark as it may seem.

Chapter Three

CLOSING THE EVALUATIVE CIRCLE: RESOLVING DISAGREEMENTS ABOUT COGNITIVE VALUES

As we have seen, the hierarchical model, when stripped of some of its more grandiose claims to have the resources to terminate every scientific controversy, looks rather promising as a model for explaining dissensus and consensus at the factual and methodological levels, especially when we factor in the bidirectionality of its justificatory structure. We have also noted some of the sorts of situations in which the hierarchical model fails to deliver a verdict. Many of these latter prove to be nonstandard or highly unusual. But there *is* a point where the model breaks down badly and repeatedly: specifically, when scientists disagree about (some of) their basic cognitive aims or goals. Since those goals are at the top of the justificatory ladder in this model, there is apparently no recourse, no court of independent appeal, when scientists differ about axiological matters. Yet differ they do. The history of science is rife with controversies between, for instance, realists and instrumentalists, reductionists and antireductionists, advocates and critics of simplicity, proponents of teleology and advocates of purely efficient causality. At bottom, all these debates have turned on divergent views about the attributes our theories should possess (and thus about the aims of scientific theorizing). The existence of such controversies, along with the fact that they often eventually issue in consensus, exposes the core weakness in the hierarchical model, for that model gives us no reason to anticipate the emergence of consensus in such circumstances, nor can it explain that consensus once it does materialize. Accordingly, the frequent closure of axiological disagreements in science demonstrates the urgency of supplementing that model with other machinery. This chapter is devoted to a discussion of some consensus-formation mechanisms at this important axiological level.

THE COVARIANCE FALLACY

Before we turn to that topic, however, we must do a bit of preliminary spadework to expose some overhasty assumptions commonly made about the connections between aims and goals, on the one hand, and claims at the factual and methodological levels, on the other. Precisely because it is natural to regard rules as means or instrumentalities for bringing about certain cognitive values conceived as ends, and because it is clear that theories are judged in the light of methodological rules, writers on science and scientific method have exhibited two related tendencies. Although both are natural and tempting, they must be recognized as questionable before we can really understand how disagreements about goals are resolved.

Both confusions arise from an overhasty extrapolation of the hierarchical model with which we have been working. Both are instances of what I call *the covariance fallacy*. Each form of the fallacy assumes that the presence or absence of consensus with respect to factual claims can be used to infer the existence of agreement or disagreement with respect to cognitive aims. One form of the fallacy (which appears frequently in the writings of Thomas Kuhn) involves the tendency to assume that major divergences of belief among scientists about theories or hypotheses (i.e., factual disagreements) ultimately point to differences at the level of aims and goals. Kuhn's well-known notion of a paradigm change illustrates the point nicely. Because (in Kuhn's analysis) every paradigm has its own metaphysics and its own set of cognitive standards or aims (which are unique to it), it follows that if two thinkers advocate different ontologies — and thus different paradigms — they must also espouse different cognitive goals. Contrariwise, if two scientists agree about the basic building blocks of the world, Kuhn is seemingly committed to their having identical sets of cognitive aims. Indeed, two scientists share a paradigm if they subscribe to the same ontology and the same axiology. So far as I know, Kuhn never imagines that there might be fundamental ontological or theoretical differences between scientists who share the same cognitive goals. Because he works constantly with a presumed covariance between these two levels, Kuhn normally takes differences at the level of basic theories as evidence for fundamental differences of aim or value. Of course, many others besides Kuhn tend to assume that divergences about matters of fact warrant an assumption of axiological differences. In chapter 4 I show in detail how badly flawed this thesis of covariance is; it is sufficient here simply to note the fact that the claim of covariance is a non sequitur. Precisely because (as Kuhn himself stresses in other contexts) cognitive values underdetermine methodological rules, and because those rules in turn sometimes underdetermine theory preference, it is entirely conceivable that two scientists may subscribe to precisely the same cognitive goals and yet advocate fundamentally different views about the furniture of the universe. Because they may, one must resist the tendency to read off a divergence about aims from every long-term disagreement about factual or methodological matters.

The second form of the covariance fallacy is the mirror image of the first. Here, one tends to assume that when scientists agree about factual and methodological matters, such agreement must have resulted from shared cognitive goals. So tight are these particular linkages often regarded that it is frequently assumed that an enterprise like science (in which agreement about theories and methods is rather commonplace) could exhibit so high a degree of factual and methodological consensus only if there was consensus at the level of aims and goals. Indeed, as pointed out in chapter 1, a key stimulus for classical sociology and philosophy of science was the conviction that scientists *must* operate with common goals, since they can reach agreement so often about the "facts." Many sociologists of the last generation saw their major role as that of identifying the norms that underwrote such factual consensus; and philosophers of that era assumed that, because scientists were often able to agree at the factual level, such agreement must issue from a prior agreement about cognitive aims or epistemic utilities. Yet a bit of reflection makes clear that the connections between consensus about values and agreement at other levels are much less tight than the covariance fallacy might lead one to imagine. It is entirely conceivable, for instance, that thinkers who subscribe to genuinely different cognitive aims might well subscribe to similar (or even identical) methodological rules; for each might believe, and believe correctly, that the rules he advocates promote his own cognitive ends.

Since one and the same set of rules may be compatible with quite divergent cognitive ends, scientists with different axiologies may find themselves agreed about the soundness of many methodological rules. For instance, scientific realists, who aim for a true account of the world, and instrumentalists, who are interested rather in "saving the phenomena," often advocate substantially the same cluster of methodological rules of theory appraisal. Both camps agree, for instance, that theories should account for a broad range of phenomena, make successful and preferably novel predictions, and generally exhibit a high degree of empirical support. Instrumentalists believe that theories that pass these tests will promote their end of saving the phenomena, whereas realists insist (often with rather flimsy arguments, as we shall see in chapter 5) that theories exhibiting these traits can be taken as approximately true and are thus conducive to realist aims. (It is just because realists and instrumentalists have often agreed about methodological rules that some philosophers, e.g., Nagel, have been led, mistakenly, into thinking that there is nothing of substance in the instrumentalist-realist controversy.[1] To infer as much is to commit yet another form of the covariance fallacy.)

As this discussion makes clear, there need be no agreement about basic cognitive values for thinkers substantially to agree about the appropriate methods of inquiry. Since scientists with different axiologies may agree on methodological matters, we can equally well see how it can happen that scientists may agree about the status of a broad range of factual claims even when they have divergent cognitive goals. It follows that it is dangerous to assume that factual or methodological consensus necessarily arises out of a deeper consensus about either methods or cognitive goals. In short, axiological differences can coexist with factual-level and methodological agreement. There is another way of putting the point: so long as it was plausible to assume that agreement at lower levels in the hierarchy betokened a basic agreement about cognitive goals, it was plausible for philosophers and sociologists to take the high degree of factual and methodological agreement in the sciences as evidence for the thesis that scientists share the same goals and values. There might be temporary differences

1. See, for instance, the discussion of realism and instrumentalism in Nagel, 1961.

about how those goals were to be interpreted (thereby explaining the outbreak of sporadic controversy in science), but the fact that scientists generally came to reach eventual agreement with one another about factual matters was widely construed as providing strong testimony to the universality of their shared values. Once we realize, however, that factual-level agreement can arise, and often has arisen, in situations where there are quite distinct axiologies at work, then we are going to be chary about regarding the frequent de facto agreement of scientists about the facts as warranting any claims whatever about their advocacy of common values.

I make these points as a reminder that resolution of axiological differences is not necessarily a precondition for reaching agreement lower in the hierarchy. Scientists could reach, and often have reached, near unanimity about which factual-level theories to accept, even in the absence of full agreement about cognitive methods and aims. Axiological consensus is thus neither a necessary nor a sufficient condition for factual consensus. (One might add, however, that it sure helps!)

Indeed, one reason that some scientific revolutions take place with great rapidity, and with relatively little reexamination of methodological and axiological questions, is precisely that a new theory sometimes emerges which is dominant with respect to all the then prevalent methodologies and axiologies. If someone can produce a theory that manages to do a better job of exhibiting the (perhaps quite divergent) attributes that the advocates of different methodologies are seeking, it will quickly win universal assent, even though the scientists who accept that theory may be able to agree on precious little else. If this seems difficult to conceive, consider a simple example. Suppose that one group of scientists attaches highest importance to theories that are empirically accurate while another puts the highest premium on conceptual clarity or elegance. Provided a new theory comes along which is both more accurate and conceptually tidier than its predecessor, that theory will quickly win broad assent from scientists, even though the yardsticks they measure it against are quite different. Anyone who imagines that scientists must first generate an axiological and methodological consensus before they can secure agreement about factual claims has simply failed to reckon with the elementary fact that people may have a wide range of reasons for doing the same thing.

But even if the resolution of axiological differences is not always a precondition for the emergence of agreement at other levels, it is nonetheless important to understand how such axiological differences are resolved, when they are. As I have already claimed, the history of science reveals over and again that the predominant goals of the scientific community have changed through time, often in deep and significant respects. If we want to understand how science works, it is clearly important to understand the reasoning processes that drive communities of researchers so far as to change some of their basic aims and goals.

Influential voices within the philosophy of science have argued that differences about goals, particularly cognitive goals, are simply not open to rational resolution. Both Karl Popper and Hans Reichenbach, for instance, have said that the adoption (or change) of a basic cognitive goal is a subjective and emotive matter which cannot be rationally negotiated. Nor should this come as a surprise to anyone who realizes just how influential the hierarchical model of rationality has been, for (as noted before) that model leaves basic questions of goals or values perched precariously at the top of the justificatory ladder. If one combines this view that goals are not open to rational deliberation with the thesis of Thomas Kuhn that paradigm conflict inevitably involves debate between scientists with divergent goals and that paradigm change always involves change of cognitive goals, then we seem to be at an impasse. For if (as Kuhn insists) most important scientific controversies involve scientists with conflicting cognitive values or goals, and if (as many empiricists and positivists believed) differences about goals and values do not lend themselves to rational adjudication, then we cannot escape the conclusion that scientific controversies defy both rational resolution by the participants and rational reconstruction by later historians and philosophers.[2]

But something has surely gone wrong here. The history of science does not generally appear to be the history of factions arbitrarily banished from science. In most scientific controversies, the proponents of the losing side come eventually, and often enthusiastically, to embrace the views, and sometimes even the aims, of the victors—scarcely what we would expect if their "conversion" were forced or strained. What

2. It is more than a little ironic that many of those philosophers who have been most vocal in their condemnation of relativism (e.g., Popper, Lakatos) have subscribed to the view that the selection of goals and methods is a matter of largely unreasoned conventions. A relativism with respect to aims is at least as debilitating as (and probably itself entails) a relativism with respect to knowledge.

we can say, at a minimum, is that scientists perceive themselves as resolving most controversies in a logical and reasonable way, even when those controversies seem to result from divergent views about the aims and values of science. It would be helpful to understand the basis for this perception of scientists and, equally, to see whether this perception has any rationale in a normative account of scientific activity. Finally, we want to see what these unforced conversions imply for those who simultaneously insist on the ubiquity of value considerations in scientific life and on the nonresolvability (in rational terms) of disagreements grounded in rival values.

A natural, because well-known, entry point into this discussion is Karl Popper's influential discussion of the nature of scientific aims or values in his *Logic of Scientific Discovery*. Far more than most philosophers of science, Popper stressed from early on the centrality of cognitive goals or aims in an account of scientific rationality. Popper understood that aims play a key role in justifying methodological rules, precisely because such rules are intended as means to the ends specified in our vision of the aims of science. Although Popper did not address at length the question as to how disagreements about cognitive goals in general are resolved, he did have something to say about the issue which is worth recalling, if only to illustrate the magnitude of the problem facing us.

Popper often contrasted his own view of the aims of science (roughly, those of an epistemic realist) with the views of instrumentalists, conventionalists, pragmatists, and other nonrealists. To reduce the contrast to its barest essentials, Popper believed that the aim of science was to develop ever truer theories about the world; certain philosophers and scientists rejected this value and insisted that science aimed at (say) conceptual economy, predictive accuracy, or manipulative simplicity. As Popper saw it, there was no definitive or rational way to choose between realism and instrumentalism. Both positions were, he believed, internally consistent accounts of science. Each had its own panoply of methods (albeit, as noted above, with some overlap between them); each set was selected with a view to achieving the respective aims in question. Popper generally inclined to the view that, short of demonstrating an internal inconsistency in someone's aims or values, there were no reasonable grounds for expecting the advocates of any set of cognitive goals to abandon those goals, let alone to adopt a rival set.[3] With Popper, as with most of the logical empiricists, it ultimately reduced to an irresolvable matter of taste (or, though he never defined the notion further), to "utility." Methodological rules were, for Popper, merely conventions; as Lakatos correctly noted, "Popper never offered a theory of rational criticism of consistent conventions."[4]

Popper's contemporary, Hans Reichenbach, took a similar view. Specifically, he believed that one could fault someone's methodology by showing that it failed to promote one's aims; but, like Popper, he insisted that an agent's purposes or goals, including his cognitive ones, are not a rationally negotiable matter. Some people, Reichenbach argued in *Experience and Prediction,* might have a goal of accepting beliefs that are true; others might have the doxastic aim of adopting beliefs that make them feel good. As Reichenbach described his view of the matter, "If anyone tells us that he studies science for his pleasure [as opposed to his doing science because he wants to know the truth], . . . it is no statement at all but a decision and everybody has the right to do what he wants. . . . [When we propose an aim for science, we cannot] demand agreement to our proposal in the sense that we can demand it for statements which we have proven to be true."[5] There are no objective or rational grounds, say Popper and Reichenbach alike, for choosing between rival cognitive values and their attendant methodologies (short of demonstrating an inconsistency between the one and the other).

The thrust of such arguments as these should be clear: provided that a certain set of cognitive ends or values is internally consistent, then there is no scope for a rational evaluation of those aims or for a rationally grounded comparison of those aims with any other (consistent) set. We may or may not like a certain set of goals; we may or may not share them. But these are emotive matters, quite on a par with other subjective questions of personal or sexual preference. In short, Popper and Reichenbach (along with most philosophers of science of a generation ago) fully accepted the simple hierarchical model, including its corollary that differences of aim were cognitively undecidable.

Clearly, if we accept this analysis of cognitive goals, and if we like-

---

3. See esp. Popper's discussion of the status of methodological rules and aims in the early sections of his 1959 book.

4. Lakatos, 1978, p. 144.

5. Reichenbach, 1938, pp. 10-13.

wise accept the Kuhnian point that scientists of different schools persistently endorse different cognitive goals, then we are forced to say
that the various shifts in the predominant goals in science are just part
of the history of taste and fashion, rather than part of the reasoned
and rational history of human thought. Still worse, given the centrality
of cognitive goals in the justificatory structure of every science, any
arbitrariness that infects the choice of cognitive goals will raise real
doubts about the credentials of the factual claims of the sciences parasitic on those goals. If no set of (consistent) cognitive goals can legitimately be held to be rationally preferable to any other, we seem forced
to face the prospect that there may be indefinitely many alternative
forms of "science," each tailored to meet different ends and each
entirely legitimate in its own right. In short, radical relativism about
science seems to be an inevitable corollary of accepting (*a*) that different scientists have different goals, (*b*) that there is no rational deliberation possible about the suitability of different goals, and (*c*) that goals,
methods, and factual claims invariably come in covariant clusters.

But here a crucial flaw appears, for what is being assumed is that a
rational choice between alternative sets of internally consistent sets of
cognitive goals is always impossible. This assumption, I believe, is
false, not always, but in a sufficiently large range of cases so as to make
its general espousal highly misleading. It is false because, to make a
long story unconscionably short, there is a wide array of critical tools
which we can utilize for the rational assessment of a group of cognitive
aims or goals. Once one realizes how extensive that tool kit is, it will
become clear that we are driven to none of the consequences outlined
above, provided only that we are prepared to make some major
changes in the hierarchical model.

THE RETICULATED MODEL AND THE MECHANICS OF
GOAL EVALUATION

I want to flesh out that ambitious claim by identifying two general
modes of criticizing a proposed cognitive goal or set of goals (apart
from charging it with inconsistency). I will show that one may argue
against a goal on the grounds (i) that it is utopian or unrealizable or
(ii) that it fails to accord with the values implicit in the communal
practices and judgments we endorse. These maneuvers do not exhaust
the resources of axiological critique, but they are probably the most
central resources. I want to discuss both strategies at some length.

i) *Utopian values.* — When I say that a goal state or value is utopian, I mean that we have no grounds for believing that it can be actualized or "operationalized"; that is, we do not have the foggiest notion how to take any actions or adopt any strategies which would be apt to bring about the realization of the goal state in question. If, to begin with a bizarre example, someone tells me that his basic goal is to travel at velocities higher than the speed of light, or to be in two places at the same time, my response would be to say that, given the current state of our knowledge of the world and its nomic possibilities, he is aiming at the unattainable. I might agree with him that moving at very high speeds or that being in several places at once would have its attractions; but, since I have compelling evidence to suggest that both aims are completely beyond anything we could hope to achieve, indeed since both fall in the range of what there is good reason to regard as physically impossible, I deny that it is reasonable to hold those goals. Implicit in this assessment is the belief that the rational adoption of a goal or an aim requires the prior specification of grounds for belief that the goal state can possibly be achieved.

This proposed constraint on rationally admissible goals — although not commonly acknowledged by philosophers — should be anything but controversial. We quite customarily regard as bizarre, if not pathological, those who earnestly set out to do what we have very strong reasons for believing to be impossible. Seekers of the fountain of youth, those aiming for physical immortality, builders of perpetual motion machines, and assorted other advocates of prima facie unachievable goals are typically and legitimately dismissed as unreasonable cranks. Of course, judgments of this sort, like all other judgments, are fallible. More than occasionally, our background knowledge has turned out to be so flawed as to lead us to regard as logically or physically impossible what we later learned was entirely possible. But that corrigibility notwithstanding, it is at the very core of our conception of the rational and the reasonable that anything judged as satisfying that family of concepts must, in appropriate senses, be thought to be both possible and actionable. To adopt a goal with the feature that we can conceive of no actions that would be apt to promote it, or a goal whose realization we could not recognize even if we had achieved it, is surely a mark of unreasonableness and irrationality. But so soon as we grant this elementary point, a plethora of opportunities arise for the rational and critical evaluation of rival cognitive goals or values.

I call any such argument against a value on the grounds of its unrealizability a "utopian strategy." There are at least three different species of utopian strategies commonly used in scientists' arguments about cognitive goals. The first sort one might call the charge of demonstrable utopianism. We can sometimes show that a certain cognitive goal cannot possibly be achieved, given our understanding of logic or the laws of nature. We see an effective example of this kind of argument in the debates about the aim of infallible knowledge in the nineteenth century. It was pointed out that genuinely universal claims of the sort that characterize scientific laws and theories apply to far more instances than we could ever (even in principle) have occasion to observe. Under such circumstances, the idea that we could certify the truth of a universal claim by checking each of its instances appeared hopeless. Since most empiricists would countenance no other mode of authenticating scientific theories than a proof by experience, the evident impossibility of proving theories by experience more or less forced the abandonment of infallibilism as a cognitive aim.

A second variety of this axiological criticism may be found in what I call the charge of semantic utopianism. Many scientists espouse values or goals that, under critical challenge, they cannot characterize in a succinct and cogent way. They may be imprecise, ambiguous, or both. Such familiarly cited cognitive goals as simplicity and elegance often have this weakness, because most advocates of these goals can offer no coherent definition or characterization of them; indeed, it is probably not too wide of the mark to suggest that a major reason that most scientists purport to subscribe to the value of simplicity is why relatively few of them have anything very specific in mind. The imprecision of the concept allows for multiple interpretations; and in that fluid environment, almost everyone can devise a gloss on "simple" or "elegant" which he can find congenial. It should be clear why the charge of semantic utopianism, when warranted by the merits of the case, is a serious criticism of a goal, cognitive or otherwise. If someone purports to subscribe to an aim, but can neither describe it in the abstract nor identify it in concrete examples, there is no objective way to ascertain when that aim has been realized and when it has not. Values of that sort are too arbitrary to deserve any place in a rational activity. (Indeed, it is difficult to see how radically ill-defined goals could play a genuine role in any theory of action, whether rational or irrational, objective or subjective.)

A closely related form of criticism I call epistemic utopianism. It sometimes happens that an agent can give a perfectly clear definition of his goal state and that the goal is not demonstrably utopian, but that nonetheless its advocates cannot specify (and seem to be working with no implicit form of) a criterion for determining when the value is present or satisfied and when it is not. Suppose, to take a contemporary example (discussed in detail in chap. 5), someone claims to have the goal of building up a body of true theories. Moreover, let us suppose that he offers a coherent and straightforward characterization of what he means by a theory "being true"—perhaps in terms of the classic Tarskian semantics of correspondence. Under such circumstances, his goal is not open to the charge of semantic confusion. But suppose, as we further explore this person's goal structure, it emerges that, although he can define what it means for a theory to be true, he has no idea whatever how to determine whether any theory actually has the property of being true. Under such circumstances, such a value could evidently not be operationalized. More generally, if we cannot ascertain when a proposed goal state has been achieved and when it has not, then we cannot possibly embark on a rationally grounded set of actions to achieve or promote that goal. In the absence of a criterion for detecting when a goal has been realized, or is coming closer to realization, the goal cannot be rationally propounded even if the goal itself is both clearly defined and otherwise highly desirable.

All these criticisms, which one regularly finds in scientific controversies, have an obvious plausibility about them. But their obviousness ought not mislead us into regarding them as trivial. On the contrary, such criticisms as these make up one of the central mediums of exchange in the give-and-take between advocates of rival cognitive goals; and it is the adjudication of such criticism and the responses it produces which have led to the revision of some of our once highly cherished cognitive ambitions for science.

ii) *Shared archetypes: reconciling theory and practice.* — Often, the criticism of cognitive goals is focused not so much on matters of achievability or performance as on certain apparent discordances between our explicit and our implicit goals. To see the difference between the two, we need only remind ourselves that it is a commonplace of the theory of rationality that there are a variety of ways of identifying an agent's goals. Most straightforwardly, we may in effect ask an agent what goals he espouses. The answer he gives will constitute his explicit or overt axiological structure. Alternatively, and sometimes more revealingly, we may ascertain what an agent's goals are by looking at his actions and his choices. If we find a pattern in which the agent consistently acts in ways that bring about certain end results, and if we have grounds for thinking that the agent realized that these consequences would result from his actions, then we have reason to assume that the agent was acting deliberately so as to bring about those results. Those results themselves (even if they do not figure among the agent's explicit goals) may well have to be reckoned to be among his implicit goals.

A number of familiar and thorny problems arise when we attribute implicit goals or motives to agents solely on the strength of observing the consequences of their actions. For instance, an agent may be unaware of the consequences of a certain action or pattern of actions, so that what we assume to be his motive (namely, the effect of his actions) is not his goal at all. Since virtually any action has indefinitely many consequences, there is always some doubt about which, if any, of these consequences were the ones the agent intended to bring about and which were, in effect, just incidental or inadvertent side effects of his actions. But the problem of attributing aims or values to an agent on the strength of analyzing his actions is not significantly more problematic than the other primary way of getting at an agent's values, that is, by asking him to report to us about his values. Agents, after all, are not always fully aware of what their aims or goals are, and frequently the character of an agent's goals is such that, even if he knows his real aims, he may seek to disguise them from us. Indeed, it has sometimes been argued, although it remains a notorious point of contention, that an agent has no more privileged access to what his goals are than do those third parties who study carefully his overt behavior.

Fortunately, we need not resolve such issues definitively for purposes of this analysis. What is important to bear in mind is that there are often tensions between an agent's avowed or explicit goals and the goals that seem to inform his actions. Because there are, it becomes possible to criticize an agent's explicit goals by pointing out how contrary they are to the goals that evidently undergird his actions and practical judgments.

There is nothing very surprising about all of this. Folk wisdom has long recognized the possibility of friction between one's implicit and one's explicit aspirations. Proverbs like "practice what you preach," age-old parental advice like "do as I say, not as I do," drive home the fact that the aims that an agent claims to endorse are often at odds with those that apparently guide his actions. When we find ourselves in a situation where there is a tension between our explicit aims and those implicit in our actions and judgments, we are naturally under significant pressure to change one or the other, or both. On pain of being charged with inconsistency (not to mention hypocrisy, dishonesty, etc.), the rational person, confronted with a conflict between the goals he professes and the goals that appear to inform his actions, will attempt to bring the two into line with each other.

Precisely the same sort of thing happens in science. Often a scientist will find himself explicitly advocating certain cognitive aims, yet seemingly running counter to those aims in terms of the actual theory choices he makes in his daily scientific work. Still worse, as we shall see below, it sometimes happens that the dominant goals or an entire community of scientists, as voiced in the explicit accounts they give of these matters, are discovered to be at odds with the goals that actually seem to inform that community's choices and actions as scientists. Whenever a case can be made that a group of scientists is not practicing what it preaches, there are prima facie grounds for a change of either explicit or implicit values. The change may come, of course, in either area, or in both. One may retain one's professed goals and force them to shape one's practical judgments and actions; or one may adopt a new set of explicit values that accord more nearly with the one's actions and practical judgments. Whichever way it goes, the engine driving axiological change is grounded in a theory of rationality, acting to overcome a state of disequilibrium.

Because this mode of critically evaluating cognitive values is so important, I want to illustrate its workings in some detail by a significant historical example: the decision by many working scientists in the late 1700s and early 1800s to give up the view that we should seek to restrict our theories entirely to claims about observable entities and processes. This important shift in cognitive orientation was absolutely essential to the development of such theories as atomism, uniformitarianism, and natural selection. So long as people insisted, as they had through most of the eighteenth century, that science must avoid postulating entities that cannot be directly observed, theories that referred to objects too small to be observed (e.g., atoms), or to processes too gradual to be seen (e.g., uniformitarian geology or natural selection), would have to be disallowed from science.[6]

The chief source for this shift in the explicit attitudes of philosophers and scientists toward the legitimacy of postulating unseen entities was a prior shift in the character of physical theory itself. Specifically, by the 1830s scientists found themselves working with theories that, as they eventually discovered, violated their own explicit characterizations of the aims of theorizing. Confronted by that discovery, they eventually reappraised their explicit axiology. I want to spell out this process in some detail.

For almost a century after the triumph of Newton's *Principia,* both scientists and philosophers sought to draw the appropriate morals from the Newtonian success. As read by his immediate successors, Newton's achievement depended upon the eschewal of hypothetical reasoning and upon a rigid adherence to inductive generalizations from experimental data. Newton himself, after all, had stressed "hypotheses non fingo." Whether we look to the work of Maclaurin, Boerhaave, or Cotes (or any of half a dozen other leading Newtonians), we see an effort to construct a purely observational physics, chemistry, and biology, the core assumptions of which were thought to be directly derivable from experience. This effort to limit legitimate theorizing to claims about observable processes found its counterpart in the epistemology and philosophy of science of the period. While scientists were excising unobservable entities from their theories, philosophers like Berkeley, Hume, and Condillac were busy articulating an empiricist theory of knowledge.

By the 1750s, however, natural philosophers were beginning to discover that many areas of inquiry did not readily lend themselves to such an approach. The really successful theories of electricity, embryology, and chemistry of the mid-eighteenth century seemed to depend crucially on the postulation of unobservable entities. Such theories, in the nature of the case, could not conceivably have been arrived at by methods of direct extrapolation or inductive generalization from what can be observed. Franklin's fluid theory of electricity, Boerhaave's vibratory theory of heat, the Buffonian theory of organic molecules, and phlogiston chemistry constitute a typical sample of the growing set of Enlightenment theories that hypothesized unobservable entities in

6. For a lengthy discussion of these developments, see Laudan, 1981.

order to explain observable processes. Among the most controversial of these theories were the chemical and gravitational theories of George Lesage, the neurophysiological theories of David Hartley, and the matter theory of Roger Boscovich. Although working independently of one another, and differing over many substantive questions, these three thinkers had one important characteristic in common: they quickly came to realize that the types of theories they were promulgating could not possibly be justified within the axiological framework of naive empiricism. Each of these thinkers found that his scientific theories received widespread criticism because of their alleged incompatibility with the proper aims of natural inquiry.

Against Hartley, for example, it was charged that his theory about aetherial fluids in the nervous system was but one of many hypotheses, among which only an arbitrary choice could be made. Against Boscovich, it was argued that he could get no direct evidence that the forces around particles were (as he hypothesized) alternately attractive and repulsive at the microscopic distances where contact, cohesion, and chemical change occurred. Against Lesage, critics contended that his theory of ultramondane corpuscles (corpuscles whose motion and impact were supposed to explain gravitational attraction) could not be inductively inferred from experiment.

Clearly, what confronted all these scientists was a manifest conflict between the "official" aims and goals of science and the types of theories they were constructing. Their choice was a difficult one: either abandon microtheorizing altogether (as their staunchly empiricist critics insisted) or else develop an alternative axiology of science which would provide conceptual legitimation for theories lacking a direct observational warrant. All three in our trio chose the latter alternative. In short, they sought to legitimate the aim of understanding the visible world by means of postulating an invisible world whose behavior was causally responsible for what we do observe. But they realized that such a goal made no sense in the absence of methods for warranting claims about unobservable entities. Thus to make good on their proposed aims, they had to develop a new methodology for science. The method they advocated was called the "method of hypothesis" (or, as we have it nowadays, the hypothetico-deductive method). Such a method allowed for the legitimacy of hypotheses referring to theoretical entities, just so long as a broad range of correct observational claims could be derived from such hypotheses. Roger Boscovich, for example, insisted that the method of hypothesis is "the method best adapted to physics" and that, in many instances, it is only by means of conjecture followed by verification that "we are enabled to conjecture or divine the path of truth."[7] Hartley, in a lengthy chapter on scientific methodology in his *Observations on Man,* asserted that the methods of induction must be supplemented by various hypothetical methods if we are ever to accelerate the acquisition of knowledge beyond a snail's pace.[8]

The most explicit defense of the method of hypothesis came from George Lesage, whose theory had been repeatedly attacked. Euler, for instance, had said of Lesage's physics that it was better to remain ignorant "than to resort to such strange hypotheses."[9] The French astronomer Bailly had insisted, in good inductivist fashion, that science should limit itself to those observational "laws which nature reveals to us"[10] and avoid conjecturing about what we cannot directly observe. Lesage deplored the "almost universal prejudice" that hypothetical reasoning from the observed to the unobserved is impossible, and that induction and analogy are the only legitimate routes to truth.[11] He pointed out that his own theory was being widely dismissed because it "is but a hypothesis."[12]

Confronted with such attacks, Lesage was forced to play the epistemologist. In several later works, but especially in a treatise on the method of hypothesis written for the French *Encyclopédie,* Lesage began the counterattack. In brief, his strategy was twofold: first, to establish the epistemic credentials of the method of hypothesis by showing that such a method promoted legitimate aims for science; second, to show that even his critics — in their actual practice — utilized unobservable entities. Lesage, in short, agreed with his critics that his theory did indeed postulate hypothetical entities; but unlike them, he sought to show that it was none the worse for that.

He granted immediately that the method of hypothesis and subse-

7. From Boscovich's *De Solis a Lunae Defectibus* (1760). Quoted from, and translated by, Dugald Stewart, 1854-, 2:212.

8. See esp. Hartley, 1749, 1:341-351.

9. From a letter published in Prevost, 1805, p. 390.

10. Prevost, 1805, p. 300.

11. Ibid., p. 265.

12. Ibid., pp. 464-465.

quent verification can rarely establish the truth of any general conclusions. But then, as he pointed out, induction and analogy—the methods favored by traditional empiricists—are also inconclusive. What we must aim at in these matters, says Lesage, is high probability, and he indicated circumstances under which we are entitled to assert well-confirmed hypotheses with confidence. He went on to point out that the great Isaac Newton, for all his professed inductivism, extensively utilized the method of hypothesis. It is, he says, to hypothesis "without any element of [induction or] analogy that we . . . owe the great discovery of the three laws which govern the celestial bodies."[13] Generalizing this point, Lesage argued that there is an element of conjecture or hypothesis in every inductive inference that goes beyond its premises, which all except so-called perfect inductions do. Since no interesting scientific claim can restrict itself to what has been observed, concludes Lesage, it is unreasonable to make such a restriction into an epistemic aim.

Within a half century after Lesage's death, the "official" methodology of the scientific community had come to acknowledge the legitimacy of hypotheses about unobservable entities. What forced the change was a growing recognition that the explicit axiology of empiricism was fundamentally at odds with the axiology implicit in scientists' theory preferences. This recognition becomes fully explicit in the writings of Herschel and Whewell.

I have discussed this case at such length because it vividly illustrates the manner in which implicit and explicit axiological commitments can be played off against one another so as to bring theory and practice into closer agreement. The older explicit aim of a science free of unobservable entities became a casualty of the striking success of theories that postulated such entities. But although this case is more vivid than most, it represents a common mechanism for the rational adjudication of rival scientific goals.

Moreover, this episode illustrates how the existence of broad agreement about which scientific theories are the best can play a crucial role in resolving differences between thinkers with respect to the goals they explicitly profess. So long as two warring scientific factions can agree about certain instances of exemplary science (and is there a situation

13. This quotation is from Lesage's "Premier Mémoire sur la Méthode d'Hypothèse," published posthumously in Prevost, 1804, par. 23.

where scientists are completely unable to agree about some such examples?), those examples can be brought to bear in examining the conflicting goals to which the factions explicitly subscribe. If one of the two parties happens to be insisting on a certain goal that the shared exemplars fail to exhibit, then there is a prima facie case for rejecting the goal in question, precisely because it is not realized by (what all parties to the dispute agree is) a good scientific theory. Of course, it is always possible that, confronted with this conflict between implicit and explicit goals, certain scientists will choose to retain their explicit aims and to reject as illegitimate what they had previously regarded as an ideal example of sound scientific practice. (In the historical example cited above, several late eighteenth-century thinkers were prepared to do exactly that, even to the point of rejecting large parts of Newtonian physics because it did not exemplify their explicit values.) But unless scientists are prepared to go that far (and in the overwhelming number of cases they are not prepared to renounce the major scientific achievements of their predecessors when they have nothing with which to replace them), it remains a compelling argument against a proposed cognitive aim if the primary theories of a discipline fail to exemplify it.

There is yet another way in which scientific standards come to be reasonably abandoned, even if the process is as much by default as by design. Such abandonment occurs when scientists discover that, despite persistent and arduous efforts, they can produce no theories that manage to exemplify those standards or ideals. Consider, for instance, the fate of the demand for intelligibility or cogency of conception, in the wake of Newton's *Principia*. Until Newton's day, natural philosophers had generally insisted that our explanatory principles must have a conceptual accessibility about them. The whole point about scientific explanation, it was said, was to explain the less intelligible by the more intelligible. The idea of explaining the world by postulating entities and processes which were even more obscurely understood was anathema to the mainstream intellectual traditions of the West. Shortly before Newton's time, this explanatory ideal had been described at length by Descartes, who insisted that our explanatory concepts must be both clear and distinct. Descartes, of course, had singled out the idea of action at a distance as an archetypal example of an obscure concept, which had no place in the explanatory repertoire of the working scientist. Barely had this dismissal of action at a distance become the orthodoxy, when Newton came along, arguing that gravitation was to be the primary explainer for planetary astronomy. Cartesians were aghast, and many of them spent decades objecting to Newtonian physics on the grounds that its explanations failed to satisfy basic demands of clarity and intelligibility. More to the point, several generations of Cartesians, including Huygens and numerous Bernoullis, devoted themselves to devising a physics as empirically adequate as Newton's, which could avoid offensive concepts like gravitation. As everyone knows, they nearly succeeded in this effort to produce a purely contact-action physics that could enjoy the empirical support that Newton's could claim.

But even more important to the demise of Cartesian physics than its lackluster empirical record was the growing recognition, made explicit by both Locke and Maupertuis, that several key Cartesian explanatory concepts such as contact action were every bit as obscure and unintelligible as gravitation. By the 1740s Cartesianism had largely run out of steam, or at least had run out of influential advocates, because it was no longer convincing to argue that Cartesian physics was more intelligible than Newton's. What evidently happened in this instance was that the goal or standard of intelligibility was itself a casualty of this encounter, because none of the existing theories of physics, despite serious efforts to clean them up conceptually, had been expunged of all offending concepts. Some few scientists might continue to subscribe to intelligibility as an ideal, but it ceased to be an appropriate requirement to impose on the physical hypotheses of the day because none of the extant theories showed any signs of being modifiable so as to be made fully intelligible, as that concept was then understood. This sort of situation is simply another variety of the process of goal revision via an examination of what our best (or, here, what all our available) theories seem to be capable of achieving.

We cannot end our discussion of this matter without stressing that the two general modes of goal evaluation sketched in this chapter are not cure-alls or panaceas for the resolution of all disagreements about scientific aims. It may well happen that a debate is taking place between advocates of goals which can be faulted neither on the grounds of their utopian character nor because of their incompatibility with shared examples. More generally, there are plenty of cases of axiological disagreement in which there is ample scope for fully rational individuals to disagree about goals even when they fully agree about shared examples. But that is a far cry from the familiar claim, with which this chapter began, that virtually all cases of disagreement about cognitive values are beyond rational resolution. It is crucial for us to understand that scientists do sometimes change their minds about their most basic cognitive ends, and sometimes they can give compelling arguments outlining the reasons for such changes. In this regard, disagreements about goals are exactly on a par with factual and methodological disputes. Sometimes they can be rationally brought to closure; other times, they cannot. But there is nothing about the nature of cognitive goals which makes them intrinsically immune to criticism and modification.

THE RETICULATED MODEL OF
SCIENTIFIC RATIONALITY

The outlines of a different way of thinking about scientific decision making are now within our grasp. As we have already seen, the classical hierarchical model postulates a unidirectional justificatory ladder, proceeding from aims to methods to factual claims. That model has taken us only so far toward understanding the argumentative strategies open to scientists. As chapter 2 makes clear, we must change the hierarchical model by insisting that our factual beliefs drastically shape our views about which sorts of methods are viable, and about which sorts of methods do in fact promote which sorts of aims. But our discussion here shows that more drastic changes are needed. Specifically, we need to replace the hierarchical picture with what we might call a reticulated model of justification. The reticulational approach shows that we can use our knowledge of the available methods of inquiry as a tool for assessing the viability of proposed cognitive aims. (For instance, we may be able to show that there is no known method for achieving a particular aim, and thus that the aim is not realizable.) Equally, the reticulated picture insists that our judgments about which theories are sound can be played off against our explicit axiologies in order to reveal tensions between our implicit and our explicit value structures.

Where the reticulational picture differs most fundamentally from the hierarchical one is in the insistence that there is a complex process of mutual adjustment and mutual justification going on among all three levels of scientific commitment. Justification flows upward as well as downward in the hierarchy, linking aims, methods, and factual claims. No longer should we regard any one of these levels as privileged or primary or more fundamental than the others. Axiology, methodology, and factual claims are inevitably intertwined in relations of mutual dependency. The pecking order implicit in the hierarchical approach must give way to a kind of leveling principle that emphasizes the patterns of mutual dependence between these various levels. (See fig. 2.)

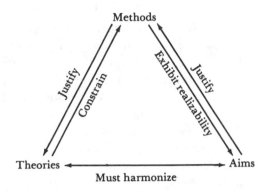

Fig. 2. The Triadic Network of Justification

It may seem to the skeptical reader that the constraints on goals proposed in the reticulational model are very weak, so much so that many different sets of cognitive goals may well satisfy them. Doubtless a wide range of cognitive goals or values can satisfy the demands laid down here. In one sense, that is good news, for if only one set complies with these constraints, and if these principles are taken to define a minimal form of rationality, then there can never be legitimate grounds for scientists to disagree about standards. And that, in turn, would mean that all those occasions when scientists have disagreed about standards in the past reflected massive amounts of irrationality in science. The bad news, or so it will be regarded by some, is that several different, even mutually incompatible, goals may satisfy these constraints. Those who want a highly ambitious theory of scientific rationality will probably ask: "But how does the reticulational analysis tell us which among the surviving goals is the right one?" I have no answer to give to that question, but I hasten to add that the question itself rests on illicit presuppositions. There is no single "right" goal for inquiry because it is evidently legitimate to engage in inquiry for a wide variety of reasons and with a wide variety of purposes. Those who imagine that that there is a single axiology that can or should guide investigation into nature have failed to come to terms with the palpable diversity of the potential ends and uses of inquiry.

To say as much is not, however, to take the bite out of the demand for rationality. If all the reticulational picture could establish about scientific rationality was that it amounted to goal-directed behavior, then we would indeed have failed, for there are plenty of purposive activities which nonetheless fail to meet our intuitive standards of rationality. Before a purposive action can qualify as rational, its central aims must be scrutinized—in ways outlined above—to see whether they satisfy the relevant constraints. But beyond demanding that our cognitive goals must reflect our best beliefs about what is and what is not possible, that our methods must stand in an appropriate relation to our goals, and that our implicit and explicit values must be synchronized, there is little more that the theory of rationality can demand.

Lest anyone think that these constraints are so weak as to exclude virtually no serious options, I hasten to add that many of the most familiar cognitive goals arguably fail to satisfy even these modest demands. Indeed, I daresay that little of the axiology of contemporary scientific epistemology would survive scrutiny utilizing these relatively mild constraints. If there are doubts on this score, recall some of the historical examples I have discussed, where central and pervasive cognitive aims were given up in the face of evidence about their unrealizability. Should those historical cases still remain uncompelling, I attempt to show in detail in chapter 5 how one can bring the machinery of the reticulational model to bear on an assessment of some well-known proposals from our own time about the proper axiology for science.

Shifting aims and scientific progress. —The argument of this chapter is thoroughly Heraclitean: theories change, methods change, and central cognitive values shift. The reader may well be wondering how, if all these ingredients are potentially in flux, if nothing can be taken as a permanent fixture on the scientific scene, it remains meaningful to talk about scientific progress. After all, progress makes sense only if it is progress toward the satisfaction of a goal or aim. If our aims themselves change, then progress itself seems to be a casualty of this analysis, for actions that promote one aim may well fail to promote a rival.

How, it might be asked, can we speak of science making progress if the very goals that constitute the axiology of science themselves shift? Such rhetorical questions seem difficult to answer. But the difficulties of reconciling the notion of scientific progress with the thesis of shifting goals are more apparent than real.

Precisely because judgments of progress are, and always have been, parasitic on the specification of goals, we can continue to speak of progress just as we always have. Does a certain sequence of theories move scientists closer to realizing or achieving a certain goal state than they were before? Then progress (relative to that goal state) has occurred. If not, then not. The matter really is as simple as that. Writers on the idea of progress (e.g., Kuhn) have failed to see this point because they seem to assume that progress must always be judged relative to the goals of the agents who performed an action (i.e., relative to the goals of the scientists who accepted or rejected a certain theory). But there is nothing that compels us to make our judgments of the progressiveness of a theory choice depend upon our acquiescence in the aims of science held by those who forged that choice in the first place. Thus we can ask whether Newton's theory of light represented progress over Descartes's optics, without knowing anything about the cognitive aims of Newton or Descartes. Instead, we can (and typically do) make such determinations of progress relative to our own views about the aims and goals of science.[14] Indeed, using these techniques we can judge the progress not only of shifts of scientific theory but even of shifts of scientific method. Does a certain methodology that displaced an earlier one stand in a more optimal relation to our own aims than its predecessor did? If so, then the shift to that methodology is progressive by our lights. All this sounds rather "whiggish," and so it should, for when we ask whether science has progressed we are typically asking whether the diachronic development of science has furthered cognitive ends that we deem to be worthy or desirable. Great scientists of the past need not have shared our aims in order for us to ascertain whether their theory choices furthered our cognitive aspirations. For these reasons, a recognition of the fact that aims and values both change does nothing to preclude our use of a robust notion of cognitive scientific progress.

14. We could, of course, utilize goals to which neither the actors nor we as observers subscribe in order to make judgments of progress, although it is not clear what use such an analysis would serve.

But if this analysis leaves us with a straightforward procedure for ascertaining whether science has made progress, it forces on us the recognition (which should have been clear all along) that progress is always "progress relative to some set of aims." Customary usage encourages us to fall into speaking of scientific progress in some absolutist sense; and we are all apt to refer (usually with much hand waving) to scientific progress, without specifying the axiology against which judgments of progress must ultimately be measured. The reticulated picture of science exhibits clearly the dangers of that mistake. Equally, this analysis underscores the fact that a particular bit of science may be progressive (with respect to one set of values) and regressive (with respect to another). There is simply no escape from the fact that determinations of progress must be relativized to a certain set of ends, and that there is no uniquely appropriate set of those ends.

Chapter Four

DISSECTING THE HOLIST PICTURE OF SCIENTIFIC CHANGE

It is now more than twenty years since the appearance of Thomas Kuhn's *The Structure of Scientific Revolutions*. For many of us entering the field two decades ago, that book made a powerful difference. Not because we fully understood it; still less because we became converts to it. It mattered, rather, because it posed in a particularly vivid form some direct challenges to the empiricism we were learning from the likes of Hempel, Nagel, Popper, and Carnap.

Philosophers of science of that era had no doubts about whom and what the book was attacking. If Kuhn was right, all the then reigning methodological orthodoxies were simply wrong. It was a good deal less clear what Kuhn's positive message amounted to, and not entirely because many of Kuhn's philosophical readers were too shocked to read him carefully. Was he saying that theories were really and always incommensurable so that rival scientists invariably misunderstood one another, or did he mean it when he said that the problem-solving abilities of rival theories could be objectively compared? Did he really believe that accepting a new theory was a "conversion experience," subject only to the Gestalt-like exigencies of the religious life? In the first wave of reaction to Kuhn's bombshell, answers to such questions were not easy to find.

Since 1962 most of Kuhn's philosophical writings have been devoted to clearing up some of the ambiguities and confusions generated by the language of the first edition of *The Structure of Scientific Revolutions*. By and large, Kuhn's message has been an ameliorative and conciliatory one, to such an extent that some passages in his later writings make him sound like a closet positivist. More than one commentator has accused the later Kuhn of taking back much of what made his message interesting and provocative in the first place.[1]

But that is not entirely fair, for if many of Kuhn's clarifications have indeed taken the sting out of what we once thought Kuhn's position was, there are several issues about which the later Kuhn is both clear *and* controversial. Significantly, several of those are central to the themes of this essay. Because they are, I want to use Kuhn's work as a stalking-horse to show how the features of the reticulational model, proposed in the two preceding chapters, can be used to produce a more satisfactory account than Kuhn offers of scientific debate in particular and scientific change in general.

Kuhn, then, will be my immediate target, but I would be less than candid if I did not quickly add that the views I discuss here have spread considerably beyond the Kuhnian corpus. To some degree, almost all of us who wrote about scientific change in the 1970s (present company included) fell prey to some of the confusions I describe. In trying to characterize the mechanisms of theory change, we have tended to lapse into sloppy language for describing change. However, because Kuhn's is the best-known account of scientific change, and because Kuhn most overtly makes several of the mistakes I want to discuss, this chapter focuses chiefly on his views. Similar criticisms can be raised with varying degrees of severity against authors as diverse as Foucault, Lakatos, Toulmin, Holton, and Laudan.

KUHN ON THE UNITS OF SCIENTIFIC CHANGE

It is notorious that the key Kuhnian concept of a paradigm is multiply ambiguous. Among its most central meanings are the following three: First and foremost, a paradigm offers a conceptual framework for classifying and explaining natural objects. That is, it specifies in a generic way the sorts of entities which are thought to populate a certain domain of experience and it sketches out how those entities generally

1. Alan Musgrave spoke for many of Kuhn's readers when he noted, apropos of the second edition of *The Structure of Scientific Revolutions,* that in "his recent writings, then, Kuhn disowns most of the challenging ideas ascribed to him by his critics . . . the new, more real Kuhn who emerges . . . [is] but a pale reflection of the old, revolutionary Kuhn" (Musgrave, 1980, p. 51).

interact. In short, every paradigm will make certain claims about what populates the world. Such ontological claims mark that paradigm off from others, since each paradigm is thought to postulate entities and modes of interaction which differentiate it from other paradigms. Second, a paradigm will specify the appropriate methods, techniques, and tools of inquiry for studying the objects in the relevant domain of application. Just as different paradigms have different ontologies, so they involve substantially different methodologies. (Consider, for instance, the very different methods of research and theory evaluation associated with behaviorism and cognitive psychology respectively.) These methodological commitments are persistent ones, and they characterize the paradigm throughout its history. Finally, the proponents of different paradigms will, according to Kuhn, espouse different sets of cognitive goals or ideals. Although the partisans of two paradigms may (and usually do) share some aims in common, Kuhn insists that the goals are not fully overlapping between followers of rival paradigms. Indeed, to accept a paradigm is, for Kuhn, to subscribe to a complex of cognitive values which the proponents of no other paradigm accept fully.

Paradigm change, on this account, clearly represents a break of great magnitude. To trade in one paradigm for another is to involve oneself in changes at each of the three levels defined in chapter 2 above. We give up one ontology for another, one methodology for another, and one set of cognitive goals for another. Moreover, according to Kuhn, this change is *simultaneous* rather than *sequential*. It is worth observing in passing that, for all Kuhn's vitriol about the impoverishment of older models of scientific rationality, there are several quite striking similarities between the classical version of the hierarchical model and Kuhn's alternative to it. Both lay central stress on the justificatory interactions between claims at the factual, methodological, and axiological levels. Both emphasize the centrality of values and standards as providing criteria of choice between rival views lower in the hierarchy. Where Kuhn breaks, and breaks radically, with the tradition is in his insistence that rationality must be relativized to choices within a paradigm rather than choices between paradigms. Whereas the older account of the hierarchical model had generally supposed that core axiological and methodological commitments would typically be common property across the sciences of an epoch, Kuhn asserts that there are methodological and axiological discrepancies between any two paradigms. Indeed (as we shall see below), one of the core failings of Kuhn's position is that it so fully internalizes the classical hierarchical approach that, whenever the latter breaks down (as it certainly does in grappling with interparadigmatic debate, or any other sort of disagreement involving conflicting goals), Kuhn's approach has nothing more to offer concerning the possibility of rational choices.[2]

For now, however, the immediate point to stress is that Kuhn portrays paradigm changes in ways that make them seem to be abrupt and global ruptures in the life of a scientific community. So great is this supposed transition that several of Kuhn's critics have charged that, despite Kuhn's proclaimed intentions to the contrary, his analysis inevitably turns scientific change into a nonrational or irrational process. In part, but only in part, it is Kuhn's infelicitous terminology that produces this impression. Notoriously, he speaks of the acceptance of a new paradigm as a "conversion experience,"[3] conjuring up a picture of the scientific revolutionary as a born-again Christian, long on zeal and short on argument. At other times he likens paradigm change to an "irreversible Gestalt-shift."[4] Less metaphorically, he claims that there is never a point at which it is "unreasonable" to hold onto an old paradigm rather than to accept a new one.[5] Such language does not encourage one to imagine that paradigm change is exactly the result of a careful and deliberate weighing-up of the respective strengths of rival contenders. But impressions based on some of Kuhn's more lurid language can probably be rectified by cleaning up some of the vocabulary of *The Structure of Scientific Revolutions,* a task on which Kuhn has been embarked more or less since the book first appeared.[6] No changes of terminology, however, will alter the fact that some central features of Kuhn's model of science raise serious roadblocks to a rational analy-

2. It has been insufficiently noted just how partial Kuhn's break with positivism is, so far as cognitive goals and values are concerned. As I show in detail below, most of his problems about the alleged incomparability of theories arise because Kuhn accepts without argument the positivist claim that cognitive values or standards at the top of the hierarchy are fundamentally immune to rational negotiation.

3. Kuhn, 1962.

4. Ibid.

5. Ibid., p. 159.

6. As Kuhn himself remarks, he has been attempting "to eliminate misunderstandings for which my own past rhetoric is doubtless partially responsible" (1970, pp. 259-260).

sis of scientific change. The bulk of this chapter is devoted to examining some of those impedimenta. Before we turn to that examination, however, I want to stress early on that my complaint with Kuhn is not merely that he has failed to give any normatively robust or rational account of theory change, serious as that failing is. As I show below, he has failed even at the descriptive or narrative task of offering an accurate story about the manner in which large-scale changes of scientific allegiance occur.

But there is a yet more fundamental respect in which Kuhn's approach presents obstacles to an understanding of the dynamics of theory change. Specifically, by insisting that individual paradigms have an integral and static character—that changes takes place only between, rather than within, paradigms—Kuhn has missed the single feature of science which promises to mediate and rationalize the transition from one world view or paradigm to another. Kuhn's various writings on this subject leave the reader in no doubt that he thinks the parts of a paradigm go together as an inseparable package. As he puts it in *The Structure of Scientific Revolutions,* "In learning a paradigm the scientist acquires theory, methods, and standards together, usually in an *inextricable* mix."[7] This theme, of the inextricable and inseparable ingredients of a paradigm, is a persistent one in Kuhn's work. One key aim of this chapter is to show how drastically we need to alter Kuhn's views about how tightly the pieces of a paradigm's puzzle fit together before we can expect to understand how paradigmlike change occurs.

Loosening up the fit. —Without too heavy an element of caricature, we can describe world-view models such as Kuhn's along the following lines: one group or faction in the scientific community accepts a particular "big picture." That requires acquiescence in a certain ontology of nature, acceptance of a specific set of rules about how to investigate nature, and adherence to a set of cognitive values about the teleology of natural inquiry (i.e., about the goals that science seeks). On this analysis, large-scale scientific change involves the replacement of one such world view by another, a process that entails the simultaneous repudiation of the key elements of the old picture and the adoption of corresponding (but of course different) elements of the new. In short, scientific change looks something like figure 3.

7. Kuhn, 1962, p. 108; my italics.

WV1 (ontology 1, methodology 1, values 1)

WV2 (ontology 2, methodology 2, values 2)

Fig. 3. Kuhn's Picture of Theory Change

   When scientific change is construed so globally, it is no small challenge to see how it could be other than a conversion experience. If different scientists not only espouse different theories but also subscribe to
different standards of appraisal and ground those standards in different and conflicting systems of cognitive goals, then it is difficult indeed
to imagine that scientific change could be other than a whimsical
change of style or taste. There could apparently never be compelling
grounds for saying that one paradigm is better than another, for one
has to ask: Better relative to which standards and whose goals? To
make matters worse—much worse—Kuhn often suggested that each
paradigm is more or less automatically guaranteed to satisfy its own
standards and to fail the standards of rival paradigms, thus producing
a kind of self-reinforcing solipsism in science. As he once put it, "To
the extent, as significant as it is incomplete, that two scientific schools
disagree about what is a problem and what a solution, they will inevitably talk through each other when debating the merits of their respective paradigms. In the partially circular arguments that regularly
result, *each* paradigm will be shown to satisfy more or less the criteria
that it dictates for itself and to fall short of those dictated by its opponent."[8] Anyone who writes prose of this sort must think that scientific
decision making is fundamentally capricious. Or at least so many of us
thought in the mid- and late 1960s, as philosophers began to digest
Kuhn's ideas. In fact, if one looks at several discussions of Kuhn's work
dating from that period, one sees this theme repeatedly. Paradigm
change, it was said, could not possibly be a reasoned or rational process. Kuhn, we thought, has made science into an irrational "monster."
   Kuhn's text added fuel to the fire by seeming to endorse such a construal of his own work. In a notorious discussion of the shift from the
chemistry of Priestley to that of Lavoisier and Dalton, for instance,
Kuhn asserted that it was perfectly reasonable for Priestley to hold onto

8. Ibid., pp. 108-109.

phlogiston theory, just as it was fully rational for most of his contemporaries to be converting to the oxygen theory of Lavoisier. According to Kuhn, Priestley's continued adherence to phlogiston was reasonable because—given Priestley's cognitive aims and the methods he regarded as appropriate—his own theory continued to look good. Priestley lost the battle with Lavoisier, not because Priestley's paradigm was objectively inferior to its rivals, but rather because most of the chemists of the day came to share Lavoisier's and Dalton's views about what was important and how it should be investigated.

The clear implication of such passages in Kuhn's writings is that interparadigmatic debate is necessarily inconclusive and thus can never be brought to rational closure. When closure does occur, it must therefore be imposed on the situation by such external factors as the demise of some of the participants or the manipulation of the levers of power and reward within the institutional structure of the scientific community. Philosophers of science, almost without exception, have found such implications troubling, for they directly confute what philosophers have been at pains for two millennia to establish: to wit, that scientific disputes, and more generally all disagreements about matters of fact, are in principle open to rational clarification and resolution. It is on the strength of passages such as those I have mentioned that Kuhn has been charged with relativism, subjectivism, irrationalism, and a host of other sins high on the philosopher's hit list.

There is some justice in these criticisms of Kuhn's work, for (as I suggest in chap. 1) Kuhn has failed over the past twenty years to elaborate any coherent account of consensus formation, that is, of the manner in which scientists could ever agree to support one world view rather than another. But that flaw, serious though it is, can probably be remedied, for I want to suggest that the problem of consensus formation can be solved if we will make two fundamental amendments in Kuhn's position. First (as argued in chap. 3), we must replace the hierarchical view of justification with the reticulated picture, thereby making cognitive values "negotiable." Second, we must simply drop Kuhn's insistence on the integral character of world views or paradigms. More specifically, we solve the problem of consensus once we realize that *the various components of a world view are individually negotiable and individually replaceable in a piecemeal fashion* (that is, in such a manner that replacement of one element need not require wholesale repudiation of all the other components), Kuhn himself grants, of course, that some components of a world view can be revised; that is what "paradigm articulation" is all about. But for Kuhn, as for such other world view theorists as Lakatos and Foucault, the central commitments of a world view, its "hard core" (to use Lakatos's marvelous phrase), are not revisable—short of rejecting the entire world view. The core ontology of a world view or paradigm, along with its methodology and axiology, comes on a take-it-or-leave-it basis. Where these levels of commitment are concerned, Kuhn (along with such critics of his as Lakatos) is an uncompromising holist. Consider, for instance, his remark: "Just because it is a transition between incommensurables, the transition between competing paradigms cannot be made a step at a time . . . like the Gestalt-switch, it must occur all at once or not at all."[9] Kuhn could hardly be less ambiguous on this point.

But paradigms or research programs need not be so rigidly conceived, and typically they are not so conceived by scientists; nor, if we reflect on it a moment, should they be so conceived. As I show in earlier chapters, there are complex justificatory interconnections among a scientist's ontology, his methodology, and his axiology. If a scientist's methodology fails to justify his ontology; if his methodology fails to promote his cognitive aims; if his cognitive aims prove to be utopian—in all these cases the scientist will have compelling reasons for replacing one component or other of his world view with an element that does the job better. Yet he need not modify everything else.

To be more precise, the choice confronting a scientist whose world view is under strain in this manner need be nothing like as stark as the choice sketched in figure 3 (where it is a matter of sticking with what he knows best unchanged or throwing that over for something completely different), but rather a choice where the modification of one core element—while retaining the others—may bring a decided improvement. Schematically, the choice may be one between

$$O^1 \ \& \ M^1 \ \& \ A^1 \tag{1}$$

and

$$O^2 \ \& \ M^1 \ \& \ A_1 \tag{2}$$

9. Ibid., p. 149.

Or, between (1) and

$$O^1 \ \& \ M^2 \ \& \ A^1. \tag{3}$$

Or, to exhaust the simple cases, it may be between (1) and

$$O^1 \ \& \ M^1 \ \& \ A^2. \tag{4}$$

As shown in chapter 2, choices like those between (1) and (2), or between (1) and (3), are subject to strong normative constraints. And we saw in chapter 3 that choices of the sort represented between (1) and (4) are also, under certain circumstances, equally amenable to rational analysis.

In all these examples there is enough common ground between the rivals to engender hope of finding an "Archimedean standpoint" which can rationally mediate the choice. When such commonality exists, there is no reason to regard the choice as just a matter of taste or whim; nor is there any reason to say of such choices, as Kuhn does (recall his characterization of the Priestley-Lavoisier exchange), that there can be no compelling grounds for one preference over another. Provided theory change occurs one level at a time, there is ample scope for regarding it as a thoroughly reasoned process.

But the crucial question is whether change actually does occur in this manner. If one thinks quickly of the great transitions in the history of science, they *seem* to preclude such a stepwise analysis. The shift from (say) an Aristotelian to a Newtonian world view clearly involved changes on all three levels. So, too, did the emergence of psychoanalysis from nineteenth-century mechanistic psychology. But before we accept this wholesale picture of scientific change too quickly, we should ask whether it might not acquire what plausibility it enjoys only because our characterizations of such historical revolutions make us compress or telescope a number of gradual changes (one level at a time, as it were) into what, at our distance in time, can easily appear as an abrupt and monumental shift.

By way of laying out the core features of a more gradualist (and, I argue, historically more faithful) picture of scientific change, I will sketch a highly idealized version of theory change. Once it is in front of us, I will show in detail how it makes sense of some real cases of scien-

Changing element   Adjudicating factors

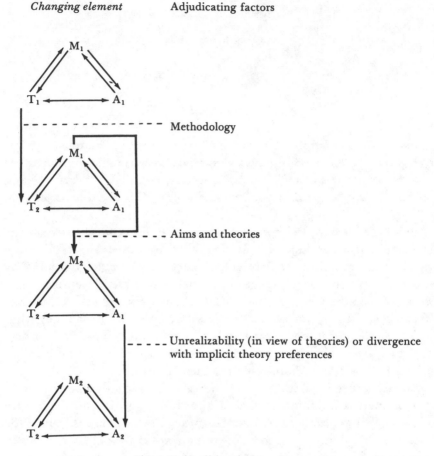

Fig. 4. Unitraditional Change

tific change. Eventually, we will want a model that can show how one might move from an initial state of disagreement between rival traditions or paradigms to consensus about which one is better. But, for purposes of exposition, I want to begin with a rather simpler situation, namely, one in which consensus in favor of one world view or tradition gives way eventually to consensus in favor of another, without scientists ever being faced with a choice as stark as that between two well-developed, and totally divergent, rival paradigms. My "tall tale," represented schematically in figure 4, might go like this: at any given time, there will be at least one set of values, methods, and theories which one

can identify as operating in any field or subfield of science. Let us call
this collective C_1, and its components, T_1, M_1, and A_1. These components typically stand in the complex justificatory relationships to one
another described in chapters 2 and 3 (and summarized in fig. 2); that
is, A_1 will justify M_1 and harmonize with T_1; M_1 will justify T_1 and
exhibit the realizability of A_1; and T_1 will constrain M_1 and exemplify
A_1. Let us suppose that someone then proposes a new theory, T_2, to
replace T_1. The rules M_1 will be consulted and they may well indicate
grounds for preferring T_2 to T_1. Suppose that they do, and that we
thereby replace T_1 with T_2. As time goes by, certain scientists may
develop reservations about M_1 and propose a new and arguably superior methodology, M_2. Now a choice must be made between M_1 and
M_2. As we have seen, that requires determining whether M_1 or M_2
offers more promise of realizing our aims. Since that determination
will typically be an empirical matter, both A_1 and the then prevailing
theory, T_2, will have to be consulted to ascertain whether M_1 or M_2 is
optimal for securing A_1. Suppose that, in comparing the relative efficacy of achieving the shared values, A_1, cogent arguments can be
made to show that M_2 is superior to M_1. Under the circumstances,
assuming scientists behave rationally, M_2 will replace M_1. This means
that as new theories, T_3, T_4, . . . , T_n, emerge later, they will be assessed by rules M_2 rather than M_1. Suppose, still further along in this
fairy tale, we imagine a challenge to the basic values themselves. Someone may, for instance, point to new evidence suggesting that some element or other of A_1 is unrealizable. Someone else may point out that
virtually none of the theories accepted by the scientific community as
instances of good science exemplify the values expressed in A_1. (Or, it
may be shown that A_1 is an inconsistent set in that its component aspirations are fundamentally at odds with one another.) Under such circumstances, scientists may rationally decide to abandon A_1 and to take
up an alternative, consistent set of values, A_2, should it be available.
(Although I have considered a temporal sequence of changes—first in
theory, then in methods, and finally in aims—which superficially corresponds to the justificatory order of the hierarchical model, it is crucial to realize how unlike the hierarchical picture this sequence really
is. That model would countenance no rational deliberation of the sort
represented by the transition from $T_2M_2A_1$ to $T_2M_2A_2$. Equally, the
hierarchical model, as noted in earlier chapters, does not permit our

beliefs at the level of theories to shape our views as to permissible methods, since justification in the hierarchical model is entirely downward from methods to theories.)

Now that we have this hypothetical sequence before us, let us imagine a historian called Tom, who decides many years later to study this episode. He will doubtless be struck by the fact that a group of scientists who once accepted values A_1, rules M_1, and theory T_1 came over the course of, say, a decade or two to abandon the whole lot and to accept a new complex, C_2, consisting of A_2, M_2, and T_2. Tom will probably note, and rightly too, that the partisans of C_2 have precious little in common with the devotees of C_1. Surely, Tom may well surmise, here was a scientific revolution if ever there was one, for there was dramatic change at every level. If Tom decides to call the view that scientists eventually came to hold "Paradigm 2," and the view from which they began "Paradigm 1," then he will be able to document the existence of a massive paradigm shift between what (at our remoteness in time) appear to be conceptually distant and virtually incommensurable paradigms.

The point, of course, is that a sequence of belief changes which, described at the microlevel, appears to be a perfectly reasonable and rational sequence of events may appear, when represented in broad brushstrokes that drastically compress the temporal dimension, as a fundamental and unintelligible change of world view. This kind of tunnel vision, in which a sequence of gradual shifts is telescoped into one abrupt and mighty transformation, is a folly which every historian is taught to avoid. Yet knowing that one should avoid it and actually doing so are two different things. Once we recognize this fallacy for what it is, we should probably hesitate to accept too quickly the models of the holists and big-picture builders. For, if our fairy story has anything of the truth about it (that is, if change is, or more weakly even if it could be, more piecemeal than the holistic accounts imply), there may yet be room for incorporating changes of methods and of cognitive values into a rational account of scientific activity. My object in the rest of this chapter is to offer some reasons to believe that the fairy tale is a good deal closer to the mark than its holistic rivals.

But before I present the evidence needed for demythologizing my story, we have to add a new twist to it. As I pointed out above, this story concerns what I call a "unitraditional paradigm shift." It reveals how it might be possible for scientists, originally advocates of one tradition or paradigm, to come around eventually to accept what appears to be a very different view of the world, not to say a very different view of what science is. I call such a change unitraditional because it is not prompted or provoked by the availability of a well-articulated rival world view. If you like, the unitraditional picture explains how one could get paradigm change by developments entirely internal to the dynamic of a particular paradigm. More interesting, and more challenging, is the problem of multitraditional paradigm shifts, that is, basic changes of world view which arise from competition between rival paradigms. To deal with such cases, we need to complicate our fairy story a bit.

Here, we need to imagine two of our complexes already well developed, and radically divergent (i.e., with different ontologies, different methodologies, and different axiologies). If we ask under what circumstances it would be reasonable for the partisans of C_1 to abandon it and accept C_2, some answers come immediately to mind. Suppose, for instance, it can be shown that the central theories of C_1 look worse than the theories of C_2, even by the standards of C_1. As we have seen, Kuhn denies that this is possible, since he says that the theories associated with a particular paradigm will always look better by its standards than will the theories of rival paradigms.[10] But as we have already seen, there is no way of guaranteeing in advance that the methods and standards of C_1 will always give the epistemic nod to theories associated with C_1, since it is always possible (and has sometimes happened) that rival paradigms to C_1 will develop theories that do a better job of satisfying the methodological demands of C_1 than do the theories developed within C_1 itself. Alternatively, suppose someone shows that there is a set of methods M_3 which is more nearly optimal than M_1 for achieving the aims of C_1, and that those methods give the epistemic nod to the theories of C_2 rather than those of C_1. Or, suppose that someone shows that the goals of C_1 are deeply at odds with the attributes of some of the major theories of science — theories that the partisans of C_1 themselves endorse — and that, by contrast, the cognitive values of C_2 are typified by those same theories. Again, new evidence might emerge which indicates the nonrealizability of some of the central cognitive aims of C_1 and the achievability of the aims of C_2. In all these circumstances (and several obvious ones which I shall not enumerate), the

10. See above, p. 43.

only reasonable thing for a scientist to do would be to give up C_1 and to embrace C_2.

But, once we begin to play around with the transformations permitted by the reticulational model, we see that the transition from one paradigm or world view to another can itself be a step-wise process, requiring none of the wholesale shifts in allegiance at every level required by Kuhn's analysis. The advocates of C_1 might, for instance, decide initially to accept many of the substantive theories of C_2, while still retaining for a time the methodology and axiology of C_1. At a later stage they might be led by a different chain of arguments and evidence to accept the methodology of C_2 while retaining C_1's axiology. Finally, they might eventually come to share the values of C_2. As William Whewell showed more than a century ago, precisely some such series of shifts occurred in the gradual capitulation of Cartesian physicists to the natural philosophy of Newton.[11]

In effect, I am claiming that the solution of the problem of consensus formation in the multiparadigm situation to be nothing more than a special or degenerate instance of unitraditional change. It follows that, if we can show that the unitraditional fairy tale has something going for it, then we will solve both forms of the consensus-formation problem simultaneously. The core question is whether the gradualist myth, which I have just sketched out, is better supported by the historical record than the holistic picture associated with Kuhn.

One striking way of formulating the contrast between the piecemeal and the holistic models, and thus designing a test to choose between them, is to ask a fairly straightforward question about the historical record: Is it true that the major historical shifts in the methodological rules of science and in the cognitive values of scientists have invariably been contemporaneous with one another *and* with shifts in substantive theories and ontologies? The holistic account is clearly committed to an affirmative answer to the question. Indeed, it is a straightforward corollary of Kuhn's analysis that changes in rules or values, when they occur, will occur only when a scientific revolution takes place, that is, only when there is a concomitant shift in theories, methods, and values. A change in values without an associated change in basic ontol-

---

11. See Whewell's remarkably insightful essay of 1851, where he remarks, apropos the transition from one global theory to another: "the change . . . is effected by a transformation, or series of transformations, of the earlier hypothesis, by means of which it is brought nearer and nearer to the second [i.e., later]" (1851, p. 139).

ogy is not a permissible variation countenanced in the Kuhnian scheme.[12] Nor is a change in methods possible for Kuhn without a paradigm change. Kuhn's analysis flatly denies that the values and norms of a "mature" science can shift in the absence of a revolution. Yet there are plenty of examples one may cite to justify the assertion made here that changes at the three levels do not always go together. I shall mention two such examples.

Consider, first, a well-known shift at the level of methodological rules. From the time of Bacon until the early nineteenth century most scientists subscribed to variants of the rules of inductive inference associated with Bacon, Hume, and Newton. The methods of agreement, difference, and concomitant variations were a standard part of the repertoire of most working scientists for two hundred years. These rules, at least as then understood, foreclosed the postulation of any theoretical or hypothetical entities, since observable bodies were the only sort of objects and properties to which one could apply traditional inductive methods. More generally (as shown in chap. 3), thinkers of the Enlightenment believed it important to develop rules of inquiry which would exclude unobservable entities and bring to heel the tendency of scientists to indulge their *l'esprit de système*. Newton's famous third rule of reasoning in philosophy, the notorious "hypotheses non fingo," was but a particularly succinct and influential formulation of this trenchant empiricism.

It is now common knowledge that by the late nineteenth century this methodological orientation had largely vanished from the writings of major scientists and methodologists. Whewell, Peirce, Helmholtz, Mach, Darwin, Hertz, and a host of other luminaries had, by the 1860s and 1870s, come to believe that it was quite legitimate for science to postulate unobservable entities, and that most of the traditional rules of inductive reasoning had been superseded by the logic of hypothe-

12. Some amplification of this point is required. Kuhn evidently believes that there are some values that transcend specific paradigms. He mentions such examples as the demand for accuracy, consistency, and simplicity. The fortunes of these values are not linked to specific paradigms. Thus, if they were to change, such change would presumably be independent of shifts in paradigms. In Kuhn's view, however, these values have persisted unchanged since the seventeenth century. Or, rather, scientists have invoked these values persistently since that time; strictly speaking, on Kuhn's analysis, these values are changing constantly, since each scientist interprets them slightly differently. For a detailed discussion of Kuhn's handling of these quasi-shared values, see the final section of this chapter.

tico-deduction. Elsewhere I have described this shift in detail.[13] What is important for our purposes is both that it occurred and when it occurred. That it took place would be denied, I think, by no one who studies the record; determining precisely when it occurred is more problematic, although probably no scholar would quarrel with the claim that it comes in the period from 1800 to 1860. And a dating as fuzzy as that is sufficient to make out my argument.

For here we have a shift in the history of the explicit methodology of the scientific community as significant as one can imagine — from methods of enumerative and eliminative induction to the method of hypothesis — occurring across the spectrum of the theoretical sciences, from celestial mechanics to chemistry and biology.[14] Yet where is the larger and more global scientific revolution of which this methodological shift was the concomitant? There were of course revolutions, and important ones, in this period. Yet this change in methodology cannot be specifically linked to any of the familiar revolutions of the period. The method of hypothesis did not become the orthodoxy in science of the late nineteenth century because it rode on the coattails of any specific change in ontology or scientific values. So far as I can see, this methodological revolution was independent of any particular program of research in any one of the sciences, which is not to say that it did not reflect some very general tendencies appearing across the board in scientific research. The holist model, which would have us believe that changes in methodological orientation are invariably linked to changes in values and ontology, is patently mistaken here. Nor, if one reflects on the nature of methodological discussion, should we have expected otherwise. As noted in chapter 2, methodological rules can reasonably be criticized and altered if one discovers that they fail optimally to promote our cognitive aims. If our aims shift, as they would in a Kuhnian paradigm shift, we would of course expect a reappraisal of our methods of inquiry in light of their suitability for promoting the new goals. But, even when our goals shift not at all, we sometimes discover arguments and evidence which indicate that the methods we have been using all along are not really suitable for our purposes. Such readjustments of methodological orientation, in the absence of a paradigm

13. See Laudan, 1981.
14. For a discussion of the difference between explicit and implicit methodology, see chap. 3, pp. 53 ff.

shift, are a direct corollary of the reticulational model as I described it earlier; yet they pose a serious anomaly for Kuhn's analysis.

What about changes in aims, as opposed to rules? Is it not perhaps more plausible to imagine, with Kuhn, that changes of cognitive values are always part of broader shifts of paradigm or world view? Here again, the historical record speaks out convincingly against this account. Consider, very briefly, one example: the abandonment of "infallible knowledge" as an epistemic aim for science. As before, my historical account will have to be "potted" for purposes of brevity; but there is ample serious scholarship to back up the claims I shall be making.[15]

That scholarship has established quite convincingly that, during the course of the nineteenth century, the view of science as aiming at certainty gave way among most scientists to a more modest program of producing theories that were plausible, probable, or well tested. As Peirce and Dewey have argued, this shift represents one of the great watersheds in the history of scientific philosophy: the abandonment of the quest for certainty. More or less from the time of Aristotle onward, scientists had sought theories that were demonstrable and apodictically certain. Although empiricists and rationalists disagreed about precisely how to certify knowledge as certain and incorrigible, all agreed that science was aiming exclusively at the production of such knowledge. This same view of science largely prevailed at the beginning of the nineteenth century. But by the end of that century this demonstrative and infallibilist ideal was well and truly dead. Scientists of almost every persuasion were insistent that science could, at most, aspire to the status of highly probable knowledge. Certainty, incorrigibility, and indefeasibility ceased to figure among the central aims of most twentieth-century scientists.

The full story surrounding the replacement of the quest for certainty by a thoroughgoing fallibilism is long and complicated; I have attempted to sketch out parts of that story elsewhere.[16] What matters for our purposes here is not so much the details of this epistemic revolution, but the fact that this profound transformation was not specifically associated with the emergence of any new scientific paradigms or research programs. The question of timing is crucial, for it is impor-

15. For an extensive bibliography on this issue, see Laudan, 1968.
16. See Laudan, 1981.

tant to see that this deep shift in axiological sensibilities was independent of any specific change in scientific world view or paradigm. No new scientific tradition or paradigm in the nineteenth century was associated with a specifically fallibilist axiology. Quite the reverse, fallibilism came to be associated with virtually every major program of scientific research by the mid- to late nineteenth century. Atomists and antiatomists, wave theorists and particle theorists, Darwinians and Lamarckians, uniformitarians and catastrophists — all subscribed to the new consensus about the corrigibility and indemonstrability of scientific theories. A similar story could be told about other cognitive values which have gone the way of all flesh. The abandonment of intelligibility, of the requirement of picturable or mechanically constructible models of natural processes, of the insistence on "complete" descriptions of nature — all reveal a similar pattern. The abandonment of each of these cognitive ideals was largely independent of shifts in basic theories about nature.

Once again, the holistic approach leads to expectations that are confounded by the historical record. Changes in values and changes in substantive ontologies or methodologies show no neat isomorphism. Change certainly occurs at all levels, and sometimes changes are concurrent, but there is no striking covariance between the timing of changes at one level and the timing of those at any other. I conclude from such examples that scientific change is substantially more piecemeal than the holistic model would suggest. Value changes do not always accompany, nor are they always accompanied by, changes in scientific paradigm. Shifts in methodological rules may, but need not, be associated with shifts in either values or ontologies. The three levels, although unquestionably interrelated, do not come as an inseparable package on a take-it-or-leave-it basis.

This result is of absolutely decisive importance for understanding the processes of scientific change. Because these changes are not always concomitant, we are often in a position to hold one or two of the three levels fixed while we decide whether to make modifications at the disputed level. The existence of these (temporarily) fixed and thus shared points of perspective provides a crucial form of triangulation. Since theories, methodologies, and axiologies stand together in a kind of justificatory triad, we can use those doctrines about which there is agreement to resolve the remaining areas where we disagree. The uncontested levels will not always resolve the controversy, for underdetermination is an ever present possibility. But the fact that the levels of agreement are sometimes insufficient to terminate the controversy provides no comfort for Kuhn's subjectivist thesis that those levels of agreement are never sufficient to resolve the debate. As logicians say, we need to be very careful about our quantifiers here. Some writers have not always exercised the care they should. Kuhn, for instance, confusedly slides from (*a*) the correct claim that the shared values of scientists are, in certain situations, incapable of yielding unambiguously a preference between two rival theories to (*b*) the surely mistaken claim that the shared values of scientists are never sufficient to warrant a preference between rival paradigms. Manifestly in some instances, the shared rules and standards of methodology are unavailing. But neither Kuhn nor anyone else has established that the rules, evaluative criteria, and values to which scientists subscribe are generally so ambiguous in application that virtually any theory or paradigm can be shown to satisfy them. And we must constantly bear in mind the point that, even when theories are underdetermined by a set of rules or standards, many theories will typically be ruled out by the relevant rules; and if one party to a scientific debate happens to be pushing for a theory that can be shown to violate those rules, then the rules will eliminate that theory from contention.

What has led holistic theorists to misdescribe so badly the relations among these various sorts of changes? As one who was himself once an advocate of such an account, I can explain specifically what led me into thinking that change on the various levels was virtually simultaneous. If one focuses, as most philosophers of science have, on the processes of justification in science, one begins to see systemic linkages among what I earlier called factual, methodological, and axiological ideas. One notices further that beliefs at all three levels shift through time. Under the circumstances it is quite natural to conjecture that these various changes may be interconnected. Specifically, one can imagine that the changes might well be simultaneous, or at least closely dependent on one another. The suggestion is further borne out — at least to a first approximation — by an analysis of some familiar scientific episodes. It is clear, for instance, that the scientific revolution of the seventeenth century brought with it changes in theories, ontologies, rules, and values. Equally, the twentieth-century revolution in relativity theory and quantum mechanics brought in its wake a shift in both methodological and axiological orientations among theoretical

physicists. But as I have already suggested, these changes came seria-
tim, not simultaneously. More to the point, it is my impression that the
overwhelming majority of theory transitions in the history of science
(including shifts as profound as that from creationist biology to evolution, from energeticist to atomistic views on the nature of matter, from
catastrophism to uniformitarianism in geology, from particle to wave
theories of light) have not taken place by means of Gestalt-like shifts at
all levels concurrently. Often, change occurs on a single level only
(e.g., the Darwinian revolution or the triumph of atomism, where it
was chiefly theory or ontology that changed); sometimes it occurs on
two levels simultaneously; rarely do we find an abrupt and wholesale
shift of doctrines at all three levels.

This fact about scientific change has a range of important implications for our understanding of scientific debate and scientific controversy. Leaving aside the atypical case of simultaneous shifts at all three
levels (discussed in chap. 3), it means that most instances of scientific
change — including most of the events we call scientific revolutions —
occur amid a significant degree of consensus at a variety of levels
among the contending parties. Scientists may, for instance, disagree
about specific theories yet agree about the appropriate rules for theory
appraisal. They may even disagree about both theories and rules but
accept the same cognitive values. Alternatively, they may accept the
same theories and rules yet disagree about the cognitive values they
espouse. In all these cases there is no reason to speak (with Kuhn) of
"incommensurable choices" or "conversion experiences," or (with Foucault) about abrupt "ruptures of thought," for there is in each instance
the possibility of bringing the disagreement to rational closure. Of
course, it may happen in specific cases that the mechanisms of rational
adjudication are of no avail, for the parties may be contending about
matters that are underdetermined by the beliefs and standards the
contending parties share in common. But, even here, we can still say
that there are rational rules governing the game being played, and
that the moves being made (i.e., the beliefs being debated and the
arguments being arrayed for and against them) are in full compliance
with the rules of the game.

Above all, we must bear in mind that it has never been established
that such instances of holistic change constitute more than a tiny frac-
tion of scientific disagreements. Because such cases are arguably so
atypical, it follows that sociologists and philosophers of science who

predicate their theories of scientific change and cognition on the presumed ubiquity of irresolvable standoffs between monolithic world views (of the sort that Kuhn describes in *Structure of Scientific Revolutions*) run the clear risk of failing to recognize the complex ways in which rival theories typically share important background assumptions in common. To put it differently, global claims about the immunity of interparadigmatic disputes to rational adjudication (and such claims are central in the work of both Kuhn and Lakatos) depend for their plausibility on systematically ignoring the piecemeal character of most forms of scientific change and on a gross exaggeration of the impotence of rational considerations to bring such disagreements to closure. Beyond that, I have argued that, even if interparadigmatic clashes had the character Kuhn says they do (namely, of involving little or no overlap at any of the three levels), it still would not follow that there are no rational grounds for a critical and comparative assessment of the rival paradigms. In sum, no adequate support has been provided for the claim that clashes between rival scientific camps can never, or rarely ever, be resolved in an objective fashion. The problem of consensus formation, which I earlier suggested was the great Kuhnian enigma,[17] can be resolved, but only if we realize that science has adjudicatory mechanisms whose existence has gone unnoticed by Kuhn and the other holists.

But it would be misleading to conclude this treatment of Kuhn and the holist theory of theory change on such a triumphal note, for we have yet to confront directly and explicitly another relevant side of Kuhn's work: specifically, his claim, elaborated through a variety of arguments, that methodological rules and shared cognitive values (on which I have laid so much stress as instruments of closure and consensus formation) are impotent to resolve large-scale scientific disagreement. We must now turn to that task directly.

KUHN'S CRITIQUE OF METHODOLOGY

Several writers (e.g., Quine, Hesse, Goodman) have asserted that the rules or principles of scientific appraisal underdetermine theory choice. For reasons I have tried to spell out elsewhere,[18] such a view is

17. See chap. 1, above.
18. See Laudan, forthcoming.

badly flawed. Some authors, for instance, tend to confuse the logical underdetermination of theories by data with the underdetermination of theory choice by methodological rules. Others (e.g., Hesse and Bloor) have mistakenly taken the logical underdetermination of theories to be a license for asserting the causal underdetermination of our theoretical beliefs by the sensory evidence to which we are exposed.[19] But there is a weaker, and much more interesting, version of the thesis of underdetermination, which has been developed most fully in Kuhn's recent writings. Indeed, it is one of the strengths of Kuhn's challenge to traditional philosophy of science that he has "localized" and given flesh to the case for underdetermination, in ways that make it prima facie much more telling. In brief, Kuhn's view is this: if we examine situations where scientists are required to make a choice among the handful of paradigms that confront them at any time, we discover that the relevant evidence and appropriate methodological standards fail to pick out one contender as unequivocally superior to its extant rival(s). I call such situations cases of "local" underdetermination, by way of contrasting them with the more global forms of underdetermination (which say, in effect, that the rules are insufficient to pick out any theory as being uniquely supported by the data). Kuhn offers four distinct arguments for local underdetermination. Each is designed to show that, although methodological rules and standards do constrain and delimit a scientist's choices or options, those rules and standards are never sufficient to compel or unequivocally to warrant the choice of one paradigm over another.

1) *The "ambiguity of shared standards" argument.* — Kuhn's first argument for methodological underdetermination rests on the purported ambiguity of the methodological rules or standards that are shared by advocates of rival paradigms. The argument first appeared in *The Structure of Scientific Revolutions* (1962) and has been extended considerably in his later *The Essential Tension* (1977). As he put it in the earlier work, "lifelong resistance [to a new theory]...is not a violation of scientific standards...though the historian can always find men — Priestley, for instance — who were unreasonable to resist for as long as they did, he will not find a point at which resistance becomes illogical or unscientific."[20] Many of Kuhn's readers were per-

19. See ibid. for a lengthy treatment of some issues surrounding underdetermination of theories.
20. Kuhn, 1962, p. 159.

plexed by the juxtaposition of claims in such passages as these. On the one hand, we are told that Priestley's continued refusal to accept the theory of Lavoisier was "unreasonable"; but we are also told that Priestley's refusal was neither "illogical" nor "unscientific." To those inclined to think that being "scientific" (at least in the usual sense of that term) required one to be "reasonable" about shaping one's beliefs, Kuhn seemed to be talking gibberish. On a more sympathetic construal, Kuhn seemed to be saying that a scientist could always interpret the applicable standards of appraisal, whatever they might be, so as to "rationalize" his own paradigmatic preferences, whatever they might be. This amounts to claiming that the methodological rules or standards of science never make a real or decisive difference to the outcome of a process of theory choice; if any set of rules can be used to justify any theory whatever, then methodology would seem to amount to just so much window dressing. But that construal, it turns out, is a far cry from what Kuhn intended. As he has made clear in later writings, he wants to bestow a positive, if (compared with the traditional view) much curtailed, role on methodological standards in scientific choice.

What Kuhn apparently has in mind is that the shared criteria, standards, and rules to which scientists explicitly and publicly refer in justifying their choices of theory and paradigm are typically "ambiguous" and "imprecise," so much so that "individuals [who share the same standards] may legitimately differ about their application to concrete cases."[21] Kuhn holds that, although scientists share certain cognitive values "and must do so if science is to survive, they do not all apply them in the same way. Simplicity, scope, fruitfulness, and even accuracy can be judged differently (which is not to say they may be judged arbitrarily) by different people."[22] Because, then, the shared standards are ambiguous, two scientists may subscribe to "exactly the same standard" (say, the rule of simplicity) and yet endorse opposing viewpoints.

Kuhn draws some quite large inferences from the presumed ambiguity of the shared standards or criteria. Specifically, he concludes that every case of theory choice must involve an admixture of objective and subjective factors, since (in Kuhn's view) the shared, and presumably objective, criteria are too amorphous and ambiguous to warrant a particular preference. He puts the point this way: "I continue to hold that the algorithms of individuals are all ultimately different by virtue

21. Kuhn, 1977, p. 322.
22. Ibid., p. 262.

of the subjective considerations with which each [scientist] must complete the objective criteria before any computations can be done."[23] As this passage makes clear, Kuhn believes that, because the shared criteria are too imprecise to justify a choice, and because — despite that imprecision — scientists do manage to make choices, those choices *must* be grounded in individual and subjective preferences different from those of his fellow scientists. As he says, "every individual choice between competing theories depends on a mixture of objective and subjective factors, or of shared and individual criteria."[24] And, the shared criteria "are not by themselves sufficient to determine the decisions of individual scientists."[25]

This very ambitious claim, if true, would force us to drastically rethink our views of scientific rationality. Among other things, it would drive us to the conclusion that every scientist has different reasons for his theory preferences from those of his fellow scientists. The view entails, among other things, that it is a category mistake to ask (say) why physicists think Einstein's theories are better than Newton's; for, on Kuhn's analysis, there must be as many different answers as there are physicists. We might note in passing that this is quite an ironic conclusion for Kuhn to reach. Far more than most writers on these subjects, he has tended to stress the importance of community and socialization processes in understanding the scientific enterprise. Yet the logic of his own analysis drives him to the radically individualistic position that every scientist has his own set of reasons for theory preferences and that there is no real consensus whatever with respect to the grounds for theory preference, not even among the advocates of the same paradigm. Seen from this perspective, Kuhn tackles what I earlier called the problem of consensus by a maneuver that trivializes the problem: for if we must give a separate and discrete explanation for the theory preferences of each member of the scientific community — which is what Kuhn's view entails — then we are confronted with a gigantic mystery at the collective level, to wit, why the scientists in a given discipline — each supposedly operating with his own individualistic and idiosyncratic criteria, each giving a different "gloss" to the criteria that

23. Ibid., p. 329.
24. Ibid., p. 325; see also p. 324.
25. Ibid., p. 325.

are shared—are so often able to agree about which theories to bet on. But we can leave it to Kuhn to sort out how he reconciles his commitment to the social psychology of science with his views about the individual vagaries of theory preference. What must concern us is the question whether Kuhn has made a plausible case for thinking that the shared or collective criteria must be supplemented by individual and subjective criteria.

The first point to stress is that Kuhn's thesis purports to apply to all scientific rules or values that are shared by the partisans of rival paradigms, not just to a selected few, notoriously ambiguous ones. We can grant straightaway that some of the rules, standards, and values used by scientists ("simplicity" would be an obvious candidate) exhibit precisely that high degree of ambiguity which Kuhn ascribes to them. But Kuhn's general argument for the impotence of shared rules to settle disagreements between scientists working in different paradigms cannot be established by citing the occasional example. Kuhn must show us, for he claims as much, that there is something in the very nature of those methodological rules that come to be shared among scientists which makes the application of those rules or standards invariably inconclusive. He has not established this result, and there is a good reason why he has not: it is false. To see that it is, one need only produce a methodological rule widely accepted by scientists which can be applied to concrete cases without substantial imprecision or ambiguity. Consider, for instance, one of Kuhn's own examples of a widely shared scientific standard, namely, the requirement that an acceptable theory must be internally consistent and logically consistent with accepted theories in other fields. (One may or may not favor this methodological rule. I refer to it here only because it is commonly regarded, including by Kuhn, as a methodological rule that frequently plays a role in theory evaluation.)

I submit that we have a very clear notion of what it is for a theory to be internally consistent, just as we understand perfectly well what it means for a theory to be consistent with accepted beliefs. Moreover, on at least some occasions we can tell whether a particular theory has violated the standard of (internal or external) consistency. Kuhn himself, in a revealing passage, grants as much; for instance, when comparing the relative merits of geocentric and heliocentric astronomy, Kuhn says that "the consistency criterion, by itself, therefore, spoke unequivocally for the geocentric tradition."[26] (What he has in mind is the fact that heliocentric astronomy, when introduced, was inconsistent with the then reigning terrestrial physics, whereas the assumptions of geocentric astronomy were consistent with that physics.) Note that in this case we have a scientific rule or criterion "speaking unequivocally" in favor of one theory and against its rival. Where are the inevitable imprecision and ambiguity which are supposed by Kuhn to afflict all the shared values of the scientific community? What is ambiguous about the notion of consistency? The point of these rhetorical questions is to drive home the fact that, even by Kuhn's lights, some of the rules or criteria widely accepted in the scientific community do not exhibit that multiplicity of meanings which Kuhn has described as being entirely characteristic of methodological standards.

One could, incidentally, cite several other examples of reasonably clear and unambiguous methodological rules. For instance, the requirements that theories should be deductively closed or that theories should be subjected to controlled experiments have not generated a great deal of confusion or disagreement among scientists about what does and does not constitute closure or a control. Or, consider the rule that theories should lead successfully to the prediction of results unknown to their discoverer; so far as I am aware, scientists have not differed widely in their construal of the meaning of this rule. The significance of the nonambiguity of many methodological concepts and rules is to be found in the fact that such nonambiguity refutes one of Kuhn's central arguments for the incomparability of paradigms and for its corollary, the impotence of methodology as a guide to scientific rationality. There are at least some rules that are sufficiently determinate that one can show that many theories clearly fail to satisfy them. We need not supplement the shared content of these objective concepts with any private notions of our own in order to decide whether a theory satisfies them.

2) *The "collective inconsistency of rules" argument.* — As if the ambiguity of standards was not bad enough, Kuhn goes on to argue that the shared rules and standards, when taken as a collective, "repeatedly prove to conflict with one another."[27] For instance, two scientists may each believe that empirical accuracy and generality are desir-

26. Ibid., p. 323.
27. Ibid., p. 322.

able traits in a theory. But, when confronted with a pair of rival (and thus incompatible) theories, one of which is more accurate and the other more general, the judgments of those scientists may well differ about which theory to accept. One scientist may opt for the more general theory; the other, for the more accurate. They evidently share the same standards, says Kuhn, but they end up with conflicting appraisals. Kuhn puts it this way: ". . . in many concrete situations, different values, though all constitutive of good reasons, dictate different conclusions, different choices. In such cases of value-conflict (e.g., one theory is simpler but the other is more accurate) the relative weight placed on different values by different individuals can play a decisive role in individual choice."[28]

Because many methodological standards do pull in different directions, Kuhn thinks that the scientist can pretty well go whichever way he likes. Well, not quite any direction he likes, since—even by Kuhn's very liberal rules—it would be unreasonable for a scientist to prefer a theory (or paradigm) which failed to satisfy any of the constraints. In Kuhn's view, we should expect scientific disagreement or dissensus to emerge specifically in those cases where (*a*) no available theory satisfied all the constraints and (*b*) every extant theory satisfied some constraints not satisfied by its rivals. That scientists sometimes find themselves subscribing to contrary standards, I would be the first to grant. Indeed, as argued in chapter 3, the discovery of that fact about oneself is often the first prod toward readjusting one's cognitive values. But Kuhn is not merely saying that this happens occasionally; he is asserting that such is the nature of any set of rules or standards which any group of reasonable scientists might accept. As before, our verdict has to be that Kuhn's highly ambitious claim is just that; he never shows us why families of methodological rules should always or even usually be internally inconsistent. He apparently expects us to take his word for it that he is just telling it as it is.[29] I see no reason why we should follow Kuhn in his global extrapolations from the tiny handful of cases he describes. On the contrary, there are good grounds for resisting, since there are plenty of sets of consistent methodological standards. Consider, for instance, one of the most influential docu-

28. Kuhn, 1970, p. 262.
29. "What I have said so far is primarily simply descriptive of what goes on in the sciences at times of theory choice" (Kuhn, 1977, p. 325).

ments of nineteenth-century scientific methodology, John Stuart Mill's *System of Logic*. Mill offered there a set of rules or canons for assessing the soundness of causal hypotheses. Nowadays those rules are still called "Mill's methods," and much research in the natural and social sciences utilizes them, often referring to them as the methods of agreement, difference, and concomitant variations. To the best of my knowledge, no one has ever shown that Mill's methods exhibit a latent tendency toward contradiction or conflict of the sort that Kuhn regards as typical of systems of methodological rules. To go back further in history, no one has ever shown that Bacon's or Descartes's or Newton's or Herschel's famous canons of reasoning are internally inconsistent. The fact that numerous methodologies of science may be cited which have never been shown to be inconsistent casts serious doubts on Kuhn's claim that any methodological standards apt to be shared by rival scientists will tend to exhibit mutual inconsistencies.

Kuhn could have strengthened his argument considerably if, instead of focusing on the purported tensions in sets of methodological rules, he had noted, rather, that whenever one has more than one standard in operation, it is conceivable that we will be torn in several directions. And this claim is true, regardless of whether the standards are strictly inconsistent with one another or not (just so long as there is not a complete covariance between their instances). If two scientists agree to judge theories by two standards, then it is trivially true that, depending upon how much weight each gives to the two standards, their judgments about theories may differ. Before we can make sense of how to work with several concurrent standards, we have to ask (as Kuhn never did) about the way in which these standards do (or should) control the selection of a preferred theory. Until we know the answer to that question, we will inevitably find that the standards are of little use in explaining scientific preferences. Kuhn simply assumes that all possible preference structures (i.e., all possible differential weightings of the applicable standards) are equally viable or equally likely to be exemplified in a working scientist's selection procedures. The analysis of cognitive values offered in chapter 3 shows that this assumption is ill advised.

To sum up the argument to this point: I have shown that Kuhn is wrong in claiming that all methodological rules are inevitably ambiguous and in claiming that scientific methodologies consisting of whole groups of rules always or even usually exhibit a high degree of internal "tension." Since these two claims were the linchpins in Kuhn's argument to the effect that shared criteria "are not by themselves sufficient to determine the decisions of individual scientists,"[30] we are entitled to say that Kuhn's effort to establish a general form of local underdetermination falls flat.

3) *The shifting standards argument.* — Equally important to Kuhn's critique of methodology is a set of arguments having to do with the manner in which standards are supposed to vary from one scientist to another. In treating Kuhn's views on this matter, I follow Gerald Doppelt's excellent and sympathetic explication of Kuhn's position.[31] In general, Kuhn's model of science envisages two quite distinct ways in which disagreements about standards might render scientific debate indeterminate or inconclusive. In the first place, the advocates of different paradigms may subscribe to different methodological rules or evaluative criteria. Indeed, "may" is too weak a term here, for, as we have seen, Kuhn evidently believes that associated with each paradigm is a set of methodological orientations that are (at least partly) at odds with the methodologies of all rival paradigms. Thus, he insists that whenever a "paradigm shift" occurs, this process produces "changes in the standards governing permissible problems, concepts and explanations."[32] This is quite a strong claim. It implies, among other things, that the advocates of different paradigms invariably have different views about what constitutes a scientific explanation and even about what constitutes the relevant facts to be explained (viz., the "permissible problems"). If Kuhn is right about these matters, then debate between the proponents of two rival paradigms will involve appeal to different sets of rules and standards associated respectively with the two paradigms. One party to the dispute may be able to show that his theory is best by his standards, while his opponent may be able to claim superiority by his.

As I have shown in detail earlier in this chapter, Kuhn is right to say that scientists sometimes subscribe to different methodologies (includ-

30. Kuhn, 1977, p. 325.

31. Doppelt, 1978. Whereas Kuhn's own discussion of these questions in *The Structure of Scientific Revolutions* rambles considerably, Doppelt offers a succinct and perspicacious formulation of what is, or at least what should have been, Kuhn's argument. Although I quarrel with Doppelt's analysis at several important points, my own thoughts about these issues owe a great deal to his writings.

32. Kuhn, 1962, p. 104.

ing different standards for explanation and facticity). But he has never shown, and I believe him to be chronically wrong in claiming, that disagreements about matters of standards and rules neatly coincide with disagreements about substantive matters of scientific ontology. Rival scientists advocating fundamentally different theories or paradigms often have the same standards of assessment (and interpret them identically); on the other hand, adherents to the same paradigm will frequently espouse different standards. In short, methodological disagreements and factual disagreements about basic theories show no striking covariances of the kind required to sustain Kuhn's argument about the intrinsic irresolvability of interparadigmatic debate. It was the thrust of my earlier account of "piecemeal change" to show why Kuhn's claims about irresolvability will not work.

But, of course, a serious issue raised by Kuhn still remains before us. If different scientists sometimes subscribe to different standards of appraisal (and that much is surely correct), then how is it possible for us to speak of the resolution of such disagreements as anything other than an arbitrary closure? To raise that question presupposes a picture of science which I sought to demolish in chapters 2 and 3. Provided there are mechanisms for rationally resolving disagreements about methodological rules and cognitive values (and I describe several of those mechanisms in chap. 3), the fact that scientists often disagree about such rules and values need not, indeed should not, be taken to show that there must be anything arbitrary about the resolution of such disagreements.

4) *The problem-weighting argument.* — As I have said earlier, Kuhn has another argument up his sleeve which he and others think is germane to the issue of the rationality of comparative theory assessment. Specifically, he insists that the advocates of rival paradigms assign differential degrees of importance to the solution of different sorts of problems. Because they do, he says that they will often disagree about which theory is better supported, since one side will argue that it is most important to solve a certain problem, while the other will insist on the centrality of solving a different problem. Kuhn poses the difficulty in these terms: "if there were but one set of scientific problems, one world within which to work on them, and one set of standards for their solution, paradigm competition might be settled more or less routinely by some process like counting the number of problems solved by each. But, in fact, these conditions are never met completely. The

proponents of competing paradigms are always at least slightly at cross purposes . . . the proponents will often disagree about the list of problems that any candidate for paradigm must resolve."[33]

In this passage Kuhn runs together two issues which it is well to separate: one concerns the question (just addressed in the preceding section) about whether scientists have different standards of explanation or solution; the other (and the one that concerns us here) is the claim that scientists working in different paradigms want to solve different problems and that, because they do, their appraisals of the merits of theories will typically differ. So we must here deal with the case where scientists have the same standards for what counts as solving a problem but where they disagree about which problems are the most important to solve. As Kuhn puts it, "scientific controversies between the advocates of rival paradigms involve the question: which problems is it more significant to have solved? Like the issue of competing standards, that question of values can be answered only in terms of criteria that lie outside of normal science altogether."[34] Kuhn is surely right to insist that partisans of different global theories or paradigms often disagree about which problems it is most important to solve. But the existence of such disagreement does not establish that interparadigmatic debate about the epistemic support of rival paradigms is inevitably inconclusive or that it must be resolved by factors that lie outside the normal resources of scientific inquiry.

At first glance, Kuhn's argument seems very plausible: the differing weights assigned to the solution of specific problems by the advocates of rival paradigms may apparently lead to a situation in which the advocates of rival paradigms can each assert that their respective paradigms are the best because they solve precisely those problems they respectively believe to be the most important. No form of reasoning, insists Kuhn, could convince either side of the merits of the opposition or of the weakness of its own approach in such circumstances.

To see where Kuhn's argument goes astray in this particular instance, we need to dissect it at a more basic level. Specifically, we need to distinguish two quite distinct senses in which solving a problem may be said to be important. A problem may be important to a scientist just in the sense that he is particularly curious about it. Equally, it may

33. Ibid., pp. 147-148.
34. Ibid., p. 110.

be important because there is some urgent social or economic reason for solving it. Both sorts of considerations may explain why a scientist regards it as urgent to solve the problem. Such concerns are clearly relevant to explaining the motivation of scientists. But these senses of problem importance have no particular epistemic or probative significance. When we are assessing the evidential support for a theory, when we are asking how well supported or well tested that theory is by the available data, we are not asking whether the theory solves problems that are socially or personally important. Importance, in the sense chiefly relevant to this discussion, is what we might call epistemic or probative importance. One problem is of greater epistemic or probative significance than another if the former constitutes a more telling test of our theories than does the latter.

So, if Kuhn's point is to be of any significance for the epistemology of science (or, what amounts to the same thing, if we are asking how beliefworthy a theory is), then we must imagine a situation in which the advocates of different paradigms assign conflicting degrees of epistemic import to the solution of certain problems. Kuhn's thesis about such situations would be, I presume, that there is no rational machinery for deciding who is right about the assignment of epistemic weight to such problems. But that seems wrongheaded, or at least unargued, for philosophers of science have long and plausibly maintained that the primary function of scientific epistemology is precisely to ascertain the (epistemic) importance of any piece of confirming or disconfirming evidence. It is not open to a scientist simply to say that solving an arbitrarily selected problem (however great its subjective significance) is of high probative value. Indeed, it is often true that the epistemically most salient problems are ones with little or no prior practical or even heuristic significance. (Consider that Brownian motion was of decisive epistemic significance in discrediting classical thermodynamics, even though such motion had little intrinsic interest prior to Einstein's showing that such motion was anomalous for thermodynamics.) The whole point of the theory of evidence is to desubjectify the assignment of evidential significance by indicating the kinds of reasons that can legitimately be given for attaching a particular degree of epistemic importance to a confirming or refuting instance. Thus, if one maintains that the ability of a theory to solve a certain problem is much more significant epistemically than its ability to solve another, one must be able to give reasons for that epistemic preference. Put differently, one has to be able to show that the probative significance of the one problem for testing theories of a certain sort is indeed greater than that of the other. He might do so by showing that the former outcome was much more surprising than or more general than the latter. One may thus be able to motivate a claim for the greater importance of the first problem over the second by invoking relevant epistemic and methodological criteria. But if none of these options is open to him, if he can answer the question, "Why is solving this problem more important probatively than solving that one?" only by replying, in effect, "because I am interested in solving this rather than that," then he has surrendered any claim to be shaping his beliefs rationally in light of the available evidence.

We can put the point more generally: the rational assignment of any particular degree of probative significance to a problem must rest on one's being able to show that there are viable methodological and epistemic grounds for assigning that degree of importance rather than another. Once we see this, it becomes clear that the degree of empirical support which a solved problem confers on a paradigm is not simply a matter of how keenly the proponents of that paradigm want to solve the problem.

Let me expand on this point by using an example cited extensively by both Kuhn and Doppelt: the Daltonian "revolution" in chemistry. As Doppelt summarizes the Kuhnian position, ". . . the pre-Daltonian chemistry of the phlogiston theory and the theory of elective affinity achieved reasonable answers to a whole set of questions effectively abandoned by Dalton's new chemistry."[35] Because Dalton's chemistry failed to address many of the questions answered by the older chemical paradigm, Kuhn thinks that the acceptance of Dalton's approach deprived "chemistry of some actual and much potential explanatory power."[36] Indeed, Kuhn is right in holding that, during most of the nineteenth century, Daltonian chemists were unable to explain many things that the older chemical traditions could make sense of. On the other hand, as Kuhn stresses, Daltonian chemistry could explain a great deal that had eluded earlier chemical theories. In short, "the two paradigms seek to explain different kinds of observational data, in response to different agendas of problems."[37] This "loss" of solved problems during transitions from one major theory to another is an

---

35. Doppelt, 1978, p. 42.
36. Kuhn, 1962, p. 107.
37. Ibid., p. 43.

important insight of Kuhn's; in chapter 5 I trace out some of the implications of noncumulative theory change for scientific epistemology.
But this loss of problem-solving ability through paradigm change,
although real enough, does not entail, as Kuhn claims, that proponents of old and new paradigms will necessarily be unable to make
congruent assessments of how well tested or well supported their respective paradigms are.

What leads Kuhn and Doppelt to think otherwise is their assumption
that the centrality of a problem on one's explanatory agenda necessarily entails one's assigning a high degree of epistemic or probative
weight to that problem when it comes to determining how well supported a certain theory or paradigm is. But that assumption is usually
false. In general, the observations to which a reasonable scientist
attaches the most probative or epistemic weight are those instances
that test a theory especially "severely" (to use Popper's splendid term).
The instances of greatest probative weight in the history of science
(e.g., the oblate shape of the "spherical" earth, the Arago disk experiment, the bending of light near the sun, the recession of Mercury's per-
ihelion, the reconstitution of white light from the spectrum) have generally not been instances high on the list of problems that scientists
developed their theories to solve. A test instance acquires high probative weight when, for example, it involves testing one of a theory's surprising or counterintuitive predictions, or when it represents a kind of
crucial experiment between rival theories. The point is that a problem
or instance does not generally acquire great probative strength in testing a theory simply because the advocates of that theory would like to
be able to solve the problem. Quite the reverse, many scientists and
philosophers would say. After all, it is conventional wisdom that a
theory is not very acutely tested if its primary empirical support is
drawn from the very sort of situations it was designed to explain. Most
theories of experimental design urge — in sharp contrast with Kuhn —
that theories should not be given high marks simply because they can
solve the problems they were invented to solve. In arguing that the
explanatory agenda a scientist sets for himself automatically dictates
that scientist's reasoned judgments about well-testedness, Kuhn and
Doppelt seem to have profoundly misconstrued the logic of theory
appraisal.

Let us return for a moment to Kuhn's Dalton example. If I am right,
Dalton might readily have conceded that pre-Daltonian chemistry

solved a number of problems that his theory failed to address. Judged as theories about the qualitative properties of chemical reagents, those theories could even be acknowledged as well supported *of their type.* But Dalton's primary interests lie elsewhere, for he presumably re- garded those earlier theories as failing to address what he considered to be the central problems of chemistry. But this is not an epistemic judg- ment; it is a pragmatic one. It amounts to saying: "These older theo- ries are well-tested and reliable theories for explaining certain features of chemical change; but those features happen not to interest me very much." In sum, Kuhn and Doppelt have failed to offer us any grounds for thinking that a scientist's judgment about the degree of evidential support for a paradigm should or does reflect his personal views about the problems he finds most interesting. That, in turn, means that one need not share an enthusiasm for a certain paradigm's explanatory agenda in order to decide whether the theories that make up that para- digm are well tested or ill tested. It appears to me that what the Kuhn- Doppelt point really amounts to is the truism that scientists tend to invest their efforts exploring paradigms that address problems those scientists find interesting. That is a subjective and pragmatic matter which can, and should, be sharply distinguished from the question whether one paradigm or theory is better tested or better supported than its rivals. Neither Kuhn nor Doppelt has made plausible the claim that, because two scientists have different degrees of interest in solving different sorts of problems, it follows that their epistemic judgments of which theories are well tested and which are not will necessarily differ.

We are thus in a position to conclude that the existence of conflict- ing views among scientists about which problems are interesting appar- ently entails nothing about the *incompatibility* or *incommensurability* of the epistemic appraisals those scientists will make. That in turn means that these real differences of problem-solving emphasis between advocates of rival paradigms do nothing to undermine the viability of a methodology of comparative theory assessment, insofar as such a methodology is epistemically rather than pragmatically oriented. It seems likely that Kuhn and Doppelt have fallen into this confusion because of their failure to see that acknowledged differences in the motivational appeal of various problems to various scientists consti- tutes no rationale for asserting the existence of correlative differences in the probative weights properly assigned to those problems by those same scientists.

The appropriate conclusion to draw from the features of scientific life to which Kuhn and Doppelt properly direct our attention is that the pursuit of (and doubtless the recruitment of scientists into) rival paradigms is influenced by pragmatic as well as by epistemic considerations. That is an interesting thesis, and probably a sound one, but it does nothing to undermine the core premise of scientific epistemology: that there are principles of empirical or evidential support which are neither paradigm-specific, hopelessly vague, nor individually idiosyncratic. More important, these principles are sometimes sufficient to guide our preferences unambiguously.[38]

38. Even on the pragmatic level, however, it is not clear that the Doppeltian version of Kuhn's relativistic picture of scientific change will stand up, for Doppelt is at pains to deny that there can be any short-term resolution between the advocates of rival axiologies. If the arguments of the preceding chapter have any cogency, it seems entirely possible that pragmatic relativism, every bit as much as its epistemic counterpart, is question begging.

Chapter Five

A RETICULATIONAL CRITIQUE OF REALIST AXIOLOGY AND METHODOLOGY

This essay was originally conceived as a book about how scientific theories are debated and evaluated. It is that, to be sure, but it must have become increasingly evident that it is also a book about how to judge philosophical doctrines about science. Every time a scientist seeks to justify a theory choice by citing a methodological rule, or seeks to make sense of a methodological rule by invoking a cognitive aim, he is inevitably engaging in the philosophical tasks traditionally associated with epistemology. This intimate involvement of epistemology in the workaday life of the scientist decisively gives the lie to those who imagine that scientists, especially natural scientists, have freed themselves from the age-old moorings of their disciplines in philosophy. But it is not my purpose here to argue for the blurring of any sharp distinction between science and philosophy; I have already tried to state the case for the merging of the two on numerous occasions.[1] What I do want to do in this last chapter is to flesh out the model of scientific change sketched out in earlier chapters by showing in practice and in detail how one can go about critically evaluating proposals concerning epistemic aims and methods. I claim in chapter 3 that one can criticize a cognitive goal or value in a variety of ways. The forms of criticism proposed above include (a) showing that we are not in possession of means whereby we can warrantedly ascertain whether the value has been real-

1. See esp. Laudan, 1977; also Laudan, 1982.

ized, and (*b*) showing that archetypal instances of "good science" fail to exemplify the value in question. Throughout earlier chapters my concern has chiefly been the abstract and descriptive one of modeling the way in which debate about cognitive values in science is actually conducted. But the model outlined there is intended to be more than descriptive of existing practices. It purports to give a normatively viable characterization of how discussions about the nature of cognitive values should be conducted. My object in this final chapter is to exhibit the normative force of that model by bringing it to bear critically on one of the central epistemic traditions of our own time.

Large portions of earlier chapters have involved me in a series of running skirmishes with several varieties of epistemic relativism (e.g., the thesis that cognitive aims are never open to rational adjudication, or Kuhn's belief that paradigm choice always involves personal and subjective "leaps of faith"). But these more strident versions of relativism are not the only popular philosophies of science which seem to rest on a sloppy characterization of the aims of science and of the dynamics of theory choice. Even more influential than relativism, especially in scientific and philosophical circles, is a very different version of the axiology and methodology of science — a viewpoint called scientific realism.

Indeed, a great many scientists and perhaps most philosophers (at least in the Anglo-Saxon tradition) hold that scientists, in constructing theories, should aim at giving a true or approximately true account of the deep structure of the physical world. Realists in particular argue that scientists should and do seek true theories and, moreover, that they often find them (or at least close approximations to them). Such realists as Putnam, Popper, Sellars, and Boyd have gone so far as to claim that a realist view of the aims and values of science is the only viable one. Accordingly, they have dismissed instrumentalist and pragmatic accounts of the axiology of science as impoverished and inappropriate. My purpose in this chapter is to bring the analytic machinery developed earlier to bear in examining the realist picture of the aims or values of science. Although it will be the upshot of my argument that contemporary realism fails to offer a viable account of scientific values and aims, my primary concern in discussing it at length here is to show in detail some of the ways in which the model described earlier can be utilized as a tool in contemporary epistemology and philosophy of science.

In what follows, I begin by formulating the position of the scientific realist. I next seek to show that many of the realist's proposals about the aims of science are too murky for us to implement them as scientific values, precisely because we cannot ascertain when one theory is truer than another. Leaving temporarily to one side the charge that the realist's values are unsatisfiable, I go on to show that, if we were to take seriously the proposals the realist makes about the goals and values of scientific inquiry, then we should be forced to say that some of the most impressive and successful pieces of science were (by the realist's lights) unscientific. I conclude by arguing that, quite apart from the dubious merits of realism itself, the realist's charge that the only possible values for science are those he himself proposes is a non sequitur.

But the targets of this chapter go beyond the proposed aims of scientific realism. Realists have advocated a variety of methods and rules for achieving their cognitive aims. Chief among these are two: (a) the method of "inference to the best explanation," and (b) the methodological requirement that acceptable new theories must preserve significant portions of the theoretical content (or extension) of their successful predecessors. The former rule is designed to link pragmatic success to epistemic warrant by virtue of claiming that a theory that exhibits certain explanatory and predictive virtues can warrantably be presumed to be true (or nearly true). The latter, if sound, is an important principle governing the dynamics of intertheory relations. Utilizing techniques described above, I establish that the methods typically advocated by realists have not been shown to stand in a relation to the realist's aims which would justify those methodological rules as suitable for realist axiology. In short, two principal rules of realist methodology can be shown to fail to satisfy the demands we can legitimately make of any adequate methodology of science.

1) *Convergent realism.* — Like other philosophical isms, the term "realism" covers a variety of sins. Many of these are not at issue here. For instance, semantic realism (in brief, the claim that all theories are either true or false and that some theories — we know not which — are true) is not in dispute. Nor do I discuss what one might call intentional realism (i.e., the view that theories are generally intended by their proponents to assert the existence of entities corresponding to the terms in those theories). What I do focus on instead are certain forms of epistemological realism. Put in its most general form, epistemic realism amounts to the claim that certain forms of evidence or empirical support are so epistemically probative that any theory that exhibits them

can legitimately be presumed to be true, or nearly so. As Hilary Putnam has pointed out, although such realism has become increasingly fashionable, "very little is said about what realism 'is.'" The lack of specificity about what epistemic realism asserts makes it difficult to evaluate its claims, since many formulations are too vague and sketchy to get a grip on. At the same time, any efforts to formulate the realist position with sharper precision lay the critic open to charges of attacking a straw man. In the course of this chapter I attribute several theses to the realists. Although there is probably no realist who subscribes to all of them, most of them have been defended by some self-avowed realist or other; taken together, they are perhaps closest to that version of realism advocated by Hilary Putnam, Richard Boyd, and William Newton-Smith. Although the views I discuss can be legitimately attributed to certain contemporary philosophers (and I will frequently cite the textual evidence for such attributions), it is not crucial to my case that such attributions can be made.[2] My aim, rather, is to explore certain epistemic claims and methodological rules which those who are realists might be tempted (and in some cases have been tempted) to embrace. If my arguments are sound, we will discover that some of the most intuitively tempting versions of realism prove to be chimeras.

At its core, realism is a normative doctrine about what the aims or values of science ought to be. Specifically, the realist maintains that the goal of science is to find ever truer theories about the natural world. But the modern-day realist typically conjoins to this axiological thesis a descriptive one: to wit, that the history of science, especially in recent times, can best be understood as an exemplification of the programmatic ideals of realism. For reasons we shall see below, although the normative claim of the realist is logically independent of the descriptive claim, the former is epistemically parasitic on the latter. If it should turn out that the descriptive claim is false (as I believe it is), then serious doubts will be raised about its normative counterpart, and thus about the soundness of the realist's view of the aims of science.

The descriptive version of realism usually embraces variants of the following claims:

R1) Scientific theories (at least in the mature sciences) are typically approximately true and more recent theories are closer to the truth than older theories in the same domain.

2. Nor will I claim to do justice to the complex epistemologies of those whose work I am about to criticize.

R2) The observational and theoretical terms within the theories of a mature science genuinely refer (roughly, there are substances in the world which correspond to the ontologies presumed by our best theories).

R3) Successive theories in any mature science are such that they preserve the theoretical relations and the apparent referents of earlier theories (i.e., earlier theories are limiting cases of later theories).[3]

R4) Acceptable new theories do and should explain why their predecessors were successful insofar as they were successful.

To these semantic, methodological, and epistemic theses is conjoined an important metaphilosophical claim about how realism is to be evaluated and assessed. Specifically, it is maintained that:

R5) Theses R1-R4 entail that (mature) scientific theories should be successful; indeed, it is said that these theses constitute the best, if not the only, explanation for the success of science. The empirical success of science (in the sense of giving detailed explanations and accurate predictions) accordingly provides striking empirical confirmation for realism.

I call the position delineated by R1 to R5 convergent epistemological realism (CER). Many recent proponents of CER maintain that R1, R2, R3, and R4 are empirical hypotheses which, via the linkages postulated in R5, can be tested by an investigation of science itself. They propose two elaborate abductive arguments. The structure of the first (I), which is germane to R1 and R2, is something like this:

1. If scientific theories are approximately true, they will typically be empirically successful.

2. If the central terms in scientific theories genuinely refer, those theories will generally be empirically successful.

3. Scientific theories are empirically successful.

---

4. (Probably) Theories are approximately true and their terms genuinely refer.

The argument (II) relevant to R3 is of slightly different form, specifically:

---

3. Putnam, evidently following Boyd, sums up R1 to R3 in these words: "1) Terms in a mature science typically *refer*. 2) The laws of a theory belonging to a mature science are typically approximately true. . . . I will only consider [new] theories . . . which have this property—[they] contain the [theoretical] laws of [their predecessors] as a limiting case" (1978, pp. 20-21).

1. If the earlier theories in a mature science are approximately true and if the central terms of those theories genuinely refer, then later, more successful theories in the same science will preserve the earlier theories as limiting cases.

2. Scientists seek to preserve earlier theories as limiting cases and generally succeed.

---

3. (Probably) Earlier theories in a mature science are approximately true and genuinely referential.

Taking the success of present and past theories as a given, proponents of CER claim that if CER were true, it would follow that the progressive success of science would be a matter of course. Equally, they allege that if CER were false, the success of science would be miraculous and without explanation.[4] Because (in their view) CER explains the fact that science is successful, the theses of CER are thereby confirmed by the success of science and nonrealist epistemologies are discredited by the latter's alleged inability to explain both the success of current theories and the progress that science historically exhibits.

As Putnam and certain others (e.g., Newton-Smith) see it, the fact that statements about reference (R2, R3) or about approximate truth (R1, R3) function in the explanation of a contingent state of affairs, establishes that "the notions of 'truth' and 'reference' have a causal, explanatory role in epistemology."[5] In one fell swoop, both epistemology and semantics are "naturalized" and, to top it all off, we get an explanation of the success of science into the bargain. But there is more, because the ability of realism to explain why science works is taken to provide a strong argument for the realist's normative claim that science should aim at the production of true (or truthlike) theories.

The central question before us is whether the realist's assertions about the interrelations among truth, reference, and success are sound. It is my burden in this chapter to raise doubts about both arguments I and II. Specifically, I argue that four of the five premises of

---

4. Putnam (1975, p. 69) insists, for instance, that if the realist is wrong about theories being referential, then "the success of science is a miracle."

5. Putnam, 1978, p. 21. Boyd remarks that "scientific realism offers an *explanation* for the legitimacy of ontological commitment to theoretical entities" (Putnam, 1978, p. 2, n. 10). It allegedly does so by explaining why theories containing theoretical entities work so well: because such entities genuinely exist.

those abductions are either false or too ambiguous to be acceptable. I also seek to show that, even if the premises were true, they would not warrant the conclusions realists draw from them. Sections 2 through 4 deal with the first abductive argument; section 5 deals with the second.

2) *Reference and success.* — The specifically referential side of the empirical argument for realism has been developed chiefly by Putnam, who talks explicitly of reference rather more than most realists. On the other hand, reference is usually implicitly smuggled in, since most realists subscribe to the (ultimately referential) thesis that "the world probably contains entities very like those postulated by our most successful theories."

If R2 is to fulfill Putnam's ambition that reference can explain the success of science, and that the success of science establishes the presumptive truth of R2, it seems he must subscribe to claims similar to these:

S1) The theories in the advanced or mature sciences are successful.

S2) A theory whose central terms genuinely refer will be a successful theory.

S3) If a theory is successful, we can reasonably infer that its central terms genuinely refer.

S4) All the central terms in theories in the mature sciences do refer.

There are complex interconnections here. S2 and S4 explain S1, while S1 and S3 provide the warrant for S4. Reference explains success and success warrants a presumption of reference. The arguments are plausible, given the premises. But there is the rub, for with the possible exception of S1, none of the premises is acceptable.

The first and toughest nut to crack is to clarify the nature of that success which realists are concerned to explain. Although Putnam, Sellars, and Boyd all take the success of certain sciences (e.g., physics and astronomy) as a given, they say little about what this success amounts to. So far as I can see, they are working with a largely pragmatic notion to be cashed out in terms of a theory's workability or applicability. On this account, we would say that a theory is successful provided that it makes substantially correct predictions, that it leads to efficacious interventions in the natural order, or that it passes a suitable battery of standard tests. One would like to be able to be more specific about what success amounts to, but the lack of a coherent theory of confirmation, and the notable silence from realists themselves about their explanandum, make further specificity difficult.

Moreover, the realist must be wary—at least for these purposes—of adopting too strict a notion of success, for a highly robust and stringent construal of success would defeat the realist's purposes. What he wants to explain, after all, is why science in general has worked so well. If he were to adopt a very demanding characterization of success (such as those advocated by certain inductive logicians or Popperians), then it would probably turn out that science has been largely unsuccessful (because most theories of science do not have high confirmation nor have they passed Popperian severe tests), and the realist's avowed explanandum would thus be a pseudoproblem. Accordingly, I assume that a theory is successful so long as it has worked reasonably well, that is, so long as it has functioned in a variety of explanatory contexts, has led to several confirmed predictions, and has been of broad explanatory scope. As I understand the realist's position, his concern is to explain why certain theories have enjoyed this kind of success.

If we construe success in this way, S1 may be conceded. Whether one's criterion of success is broad explanatory scope, possession of a large number of confirming instances, or conferring manipulative or predictive control, it is clear that science is, by and large, a successful activity.

What about S2, that is, the claim that a theory whose central terms refer will be successful? I am not certain that any realist would or should endorse it, although it is a perfectly natural construal of the realist's claim that "reference explains success." The notion of reference involved here is highly complex and unsatisfactory in significant respects. Without endorsing it, I use it frequently in the ensuing discussion. The realist sense of reference is a rather liberal one, according to which the terms in a theory may be genuinely referring even if many of the claims the theory makes about the entitites to which it refers are false. Provided that there are entities that approximately fit a theory's description of them, Putnam's charitable account of reference allows us to say that the terms of a theory genuinely refer.[6] On this account (and these are Putnam's examples), Bohr's "electron," Newton's "mass," Mendel's "gene," and Dalton's "atom" are all referring terms, whereas "phlogiston" and "aether" are not.[7]

---

6. Whether one utilizes Putnam's earlier or later versions of realism is irrelevant for the central arguments of this essay.

7. Putnam, 1978, pp. 20-22.

Are genuinely referential theories (i.e., theories whose central terms genuinely refer) invariably or even generally successful at the empirical level, as S2 states? There is ample evidence that they are not. The chemical atomic theory in the eighteenth century was so remarkably unsuccessful that most chemists abandoned it in favor of a more phenomenological, elective affinity chemistry. The Proutian theory that the atoms of heavy elements are composed of hydrogen atoms had, through most of the nineteenth century, a strikingly unsuccessful career, confronted by an impressive string of apparent refutations. The Wegenerian theory that the continents are carried by large subterranean objects moving laterally across the earth's surface was, for some thirty years in the recent history of geology, a strikingly unsuccessful theory until, after major modifications, it became the geological orthodoxy of the 1960s and 1970s. Yet all these theories postulated basic entities that (according to Putnam's "principle of charity") genuinely exist.

The realist's claim that we should expect referring theories to be empirically successful is simply false. And, with a little reflection, we can see good reasons that it should be. To have a genuinely referring theory is to have a theory that "cuts the world at its joints," a theory that postulates entities of a kind that really exist. But a genuinely referring theory need not be such that all, or even most of, the specific claims it makes about the properties of those entities and their modes of interaction are true. Thus, Dalton's theory makes many claims about atoms which are false; Bohr's early theory of the electron was similarly flawed in important respects. Contra-S2, genuinely referential theories need not be strikingly successful, since such theories may be massively false (i.e., have far higher falsity content than truth content).

S2 is so patently incorrect that it is difficult to imagine that the realist need be committed to it. But what else will do? The (Putnamian) realist wants attributions of reference to a theory's terms to function in an explanation of that theory's success. The simplest and crudest way of doing that is to make a claim like S2. A less outrageous way of achieving the same end would involve the weaker

S2′) A theory whose terms refer will usually (but not always) be successful.

Isolated instances of referring but unsuccessful theories, sufficient to refute S2, leave S2′ unscathed. But, if we were to find a broad range of referring but unsuccessful theories, that would be evidence against S2'. Such theories may be generated at will. For instance, take any set of terms which one believes to be genuinely referring. In any language rich enough to contain negation, it will be possible to construct indefinitely many unsuccessful theories, all of whose substantive terms are genuinely referring. Now, it is always open to the realist to claim that such theories are not really theories at all, but mere conjunctions of isolated statements, lacking that sort of conceptual integration we associate with real theories. Sadly, a parallel argument can be made for genuine theories. Consider, for instance, how many inadequate versions of atomic theory cropped up in the 2,000 years of atomic speculating, before a genuinely successful theory emerged. Consider how many unsuccessful versions there were of the wave theory of light before the 1820s, when a successful wave theory first emerged. Kinetic theories of heat in the seventeenth and eighteenth centuries and developmental theories of embryology before the late nineteenth century sustain a similar story. S2', every bit as much as S2, seems hard to reconcile with the historical record.

As Richard Burian has pointed out to me (in personal communication), a realist might attempt to dispense with both those theses and simply rest content with S3 alone. Unlike S2 and S2', S3 is not open to the objection that referring theories are often unsuccessful, for it makes no claim that referring theories are always or generally successful. But S3 has difficulties of its own. In the first place, it seems hard to square with the fact that the central terms of many relatively successful theories (e.g., aether theories, phlogistic theories) are evidently nonreferring. (I discuss this tension in detail below.) More crucial for our purposes here is that S3 is not strong enough to permit the realist to utilize reference to explain success. Unless genuineness of reference entails that all or most referring theories will be successful, then the fact that a theory's terms refer scarcely provides a convincing explanation of that theory's success. If, as S3 allows, many (or even most) referring theories can be unsuccessful, how can the fact that a successful theory's terms refer be taken to explain why it is successful? S3 may or may not be true; but in either event it gives the realist no explanatory access to scientific success.

A more plausible construal of Putnam's claim that reference plays a role in explaining the success of science involves a rather more indirect argument. It might be said (and Putnam does say this much) that we can explain why a theory is successful by assuming that the theory is true or approximately true. Since a theory can be true or nearly true (in any sense of those terms open to the realist) only if its terms genuinely refer, it might be argued that reference gets into the act willy-nilly when we explain a theory's success in terms of its truth(like) status. On this account, reference is piggybacked on approximate truth. As the viability of this indirect approach is treated at length in section 3 below, I do not discuss it here except to observe that if the only contact point between reference and success is provided through the medium of approximate truth, the link between reference and success is extremely tenuous.

What about S3, the realist's claim that success creates a rational presumption of reference? As we have already seen, S3 provides no explanation of the success of science, but does it have independent merits? The question specifically is whether the success of a theory provides a warrant for concluding that its central terms refer. Insofar as this question is empirical, as certain realists suggest, it requires us to inquire whether past theories that have been successful are ones whose central terms genuinely referred (according to the realist's own account of reference).

A proper empirical test of this hypothesis would require extensive sifting of the historical record of a kind that is not possible here. What I can do is to mention a range of once successful, but (by present lights) nonreferring, theories. A fuller list comes later (see section 4), but for now it is sufficient to focus on a whole family of related theories, namely, the subtle fluids and aethers of eighteenth- and nineteenth-century physics and chemistry.

Consider specifically the state of aetherial theories in the 1830s and 1840s. The electrical fluid, a substance generally assumed to accumulate on the surface rather than permeate the interstices of bodies, had been utilized to explain inter alia the attraction of oppositely charged bodies, the behavior of the Leyden jar, the similarities between atmospheric and static electricity, and many phenomena of static electricity. Within chemistry and heat theory, the caloric aether had been widely utilized since Boerhaave (by, among others, Lavoisier, Laplace, Black, Rumford, Hutton, and Cavendish) to explain everything from the role of heat in chemical reactions to the conduction and radiation of heat and several standard problems of thermometry. Within the theory of light, the optical aether functioned centrally in explanations of reflection, refraction, interference, double refraction, diffraction, and polarization. (Of more than passing interest, optical aether theories had also made some very startling predictions. E.g., Fresnel's prediction of a bright spot at the center of the shadow of a circular disc was a surprising prediction that, when tested, proved correct. If that does not count as empirical success, nothing does.) There were also gravitational (e.g., Lesage's) and physiological (e.g., Hartley's) aethers which enjoyed some measure of empirical success. It would be difficult to find a family of theories in this period which were as successful as aether theories; compared with them, nineteenth-century atomism (for instance), a genuinely referring theory (on realist accounts), was a dismal failure. Indeed, on any account of empirical success which I can conceive of, nonreferring nineteenth-century theories of aether were more successful than contemporary, referring atomic theories. In this connection, it is worth recalling the remark of the great theoretical physicist, J. C. Maxwell, to the effect that the aether was better confirmed than any other theoretical entity in natural philosophy.

What we are confronted by in nineteenth-century aether theories, then, is a wide variety of once successful theories, whose central explanatory concept Putnam singles out as a prime example of a non-referring one.[8] What are realists to make of this historical case? On the face of it, it poses two rather different kinds of challenges to realism: (1) it suggests that S3 is a dubious piece of advice in that there can be (and have been) highly successful theories some central terms of which are nonreferring; and (2) it suggests that the realist's claim that he can explain why science is successful is false, at least insofar as a part of the historical success of science has been success exhibited by theories whose central terms did not refer.

But perhaps I am being less than fair when I suggest that the realist is committed to the claim that *all* the central terms in a successful theory refer. It is possible that when Putnam, for instance, says that "terms in a mature [or successful] science typically refer,"[9] he means only to suggest that *some* terms in a successful theory or science genuinely refer. Such a claim is fully consistent with the fact that certain other terms (e.g., aether) in certain successful, mature sciences (e.g.,

8. Ibid., p. 22.
9. Ibid., p. 20.

nineteenth-century physics) are nonetheless nonreferring. Put differently, the realist might argue that the success of a theory warrants the claim that at least some (but not necessarily all) of its central concepts refer.

Unfortunately, such a weakening of S3 entails a theory of evidential support which can scarcely give comfort to the realist. After all, part of what separates the realist from the positivist is the former's belief that the evidence for a theory is evidence for everything the theory asserts. Whereas the stereotypical positivist argues that the evidence selectively confirms only the more observable parts of a theory, the realist generally asserts (in the language of Boyd) that the sort of evidence that ordinarily counts in favor of the acceptance of a scientific law or theory is, ordinarily, evidence for the (at least approximate) truth of the law or theory as an account of the causal relations obtaining between the entities ["observation or theoretical"] quantified over in the law or theory in question.[10] For realists such as Boyd, either all parts of a theory (both observational and nonobservational) are confirmed by successful tests or none are. In general, realists have sought to utilize various holistic arguments to insist that it is not merely the lower-level claims of a well-tested theory which are confirmed, but its deep-structural assumptions as well. This tactic has been used to good effect by realists in establishing that inductive support "flows upward" so as to authenticate the most theoretical parts of our theories. The proposed weakening of S3 would leave the realist with no warrant for giving a realist construal of the deep-structure claims of a theory—and that would be to undo realism itself.[11]

---

10. Boyd, 1973, p. 1. Boyd also says (p. 3) that "experimental evidence for a theory is evidence for the truth of even its non-observational laws." See also Sellars, 1963, p. 97.

11. Certain latter-day realists (e.g., Glymour) want to break out of this holist web and argue that certain components of theories can be directly tested. This approach, whatever its merits, runs the very grave risk of undercutting what the realist desires most: a rationale for taking our deepest-structure theories seriously, and a justification for linking reference and success. After all, if the tests to which we subject our theories only test portions of those theories, then even highly successful theories may well have central terms that are nonreferring and central tenets that, because untested, we have no legitimate grounds for believing to be approximately true. Under those circumstances, a theory might be highly successful and yet contain important constituents that were patently false. Such a state of affairs would wreak havoc with the realist's presumption (R1) that success betokens approximate truth. In short, to be less than a holist about theory testing is to put at risk precisely that predilection for deep-structure claims which motivates much of the realist enterprise.

There is, however, an even more serious obstacle to this weakening of epistemic realism. It is true that by weakening S3 to apply to only certain terms in a theory, one would immunize it from certain obvious counterexamples. But such a maneuver has debilitating consequences for other central realist theses. Consider the realist's thesis R3 about the retentive character of intertheory relations (discussed below in detail). The realist both recommends as a matter of policy and claims as a matter of fact that successful theories are (and should be) rationally replaceable only by theories that preserve reference for the central terms of their successful predecessors. The rationale for the normative version of this retentionist doctrine is that the terms in the earlier theory, because it was successful, must have been referential and thus a constraint on any successor to that theory is that reference should be retained for such terms. This makes sense only if success provides a blanket warrant for presumption of reference. But if S3 were weakened so as to say merely that it is reasonable to assume that *some* of the terms in a successful theory genuinely refer, then the realist would have no rationale for his retentive theses (variants of R3), which have been a central pillar of the realist view on intertheory relations for several decades.[12]

Something apparently has to give. A version of S3 strong enough to license R3 seems incompatible with the fact that many successful theories contain nonreferring central terms. But any weakening of S3 dilutes the force of, and removes the rationale for, the realist's claims about convergence, retention, and correspondence in intertheory relations.[13] If the realist once concedes that some unspecified set of the terms of a successful theory may well not refer, then his proposals for restricting "the class of candidate theories" to those that retain refer-

---

12. A caveat is in order here. Even if all the central terms in some theory refer, it is not obvious that every rational successor to that theory must preserve all the referring terms of its predecessor. One can easily imagine circumstances in which the new theory is preferable to the old one even though the range of application of the new theory is less broad than that of the old. When the range is so restricted, it may well be entirely appropriate to drop reference to some of the entities that figured in the earlier theory.

13. For Putnam and Boyd both "it will be a constraint on T' [i.e., any new theory in a domain] . . . that T' must have this property, the property that *from its standpoint* one can assign referents to the terms of T [i.e., an earlier theory in the same domain]" (Putnam, 1978, p. 22). Boyd says (1973, p. 8) that "new theories should, *prima facie,* resemble current theories with respect to their accounts of causal relations among theoretical entities."

ence for the prima facie referring terms in earlier theories is without foundation.[14]

More generally, we seem forced to say that such linkages as there are between reference and success are rather murkier than Putnam's and Boyd's discussions would lead us to believe. If the realist is going to make his case for CER, it seems that it will have to hinge on approximate truth, R1, rather than reference, R2.

3) *Approximate truth and success: the downward path.* — Ignoring the referential turn among certain recent realists, most realists continue to argue that, at bottom, epistemic realism is committed to the view that successful scientific theories, even if strictly false, are nonetheless "approximately true" or "close to the truth" or "verisimilar."[15] The claim usually amounts to this pair:

T1) if a theory is approximately true, then it will be explanatorily successful; and

T2) if a theory is explanatorily successful, then it is probably approximately true.

What the realist would like to be able to say, of course, is:

T1') if a theory is true, then it will be successful.

T1' is attractive because self-evident. But most realists balk at invoking T1' because they are (rightly) reluctant to believe that we can reasonably presume that any given scientific theory is true. If all the realist could explain was the success of theories that were true simpliciter, his explanatory repertoire would be acutely limited. As an attractive move in the direction of broader explanatory scope, T1 is rather more appealing. After all, presumably many theories we believe to be false (e.g., Newtonian mechanics, classical thermodynamics, wave optics) were — and still are — highly successful across a broad range of applications.

Perhaps, the realist evidently conjectures, we can find an epistemic

14. Putnam, 1975, p. 22.

15. For a small sampling of this view, consider the following: "The claim of a realist ontology of science is that the only way of explaining why the models of science function so successfully . . . is that they approximate in some way the structure of the object" (McMullin, 1970, pp. 63-64); "the continued success [of confirmed theories] can be *explained* by the hypothesis that they are in fact close to the truth" (Niiniluoto, forthcoming, p. 21); the claim that "the laws of a theory belonging to a mature science are typically approximately *true* . . . [provides] an *explanation* of the behavior of scientists and the success of science" (Putnam, 1978, pp. 20-21). Smart, Sellars, and Newton-Smith, among others, share a similar view.

account of that pragmatic success by assuming such theories to be approximately true. But we must be wary of this potential sleight of hand. It may be that there is a connection between success and approximate truth, but if there is such a connection it must be independently argued for. The acknowledgedly uncontroversial character of T1' must not be surreptitiously invoked, as it sometimes seems to be, in order to establish T1. When the antecedent of T1' is appropriately weakened by speaking of approximate truth, it is by no means clear that T1 is sound.

Virtually all the proponents of epistemic realism take it as unproblematic that if a theory is approximately true, it deductively follows that the theory is a relatively successful predictor and explainer of observable phenomena. Unfortunately, few of the writers of whom I am aware have defined what it means for a statement or theory to be "approximately true." Accordingly, it is impossible to say whether the alleged entailment is genuine. This reservation is more than perfunctory. Indeed, on the best-known account of what it means for a theory to be approximately true, it does not follow that an approximately true theory will be explanatorily successful.

Suppose, for instance, that we were to say in a Popperian vein that a theory, T_1, is approximately true if its truth content is higher than its falsity content, that is, if

$$Ct_t(T_1) \gg Ct_f(T_1),^{16}$$

where $Ct_t(T_1)$ is the cardinality of the set of true sentences entailed by T_1 and $Ct_f(T_1)$ is the cardinality of the set of false sentences entailed by T_1. When approximate truth is so construed, it does not logically follow that an arbitrarily selected class of a theory's entailments (namely, some of its observable consequences) will be true. Indeed, it is entirely conceivable that a theory might be approximately true in the indicated sense and yet be such that all its thus far tested consequences are false.[17]

16. Although Popper is usually careful not to assert that actual historical theories exhibit ever-increasing truth content (for an exception, see Popper, 1963, p. 220), other writers have been more bold. Thus, Newton-Smith writes that "the historically generated sequence of theories of a mature science is a sequence in which succeeding theories are increasing in truth content without increasing in falsity content" (forthcoming, p. 2).

17. On the more technical side, Niiniluoto has shown that a theory's degree of corroboration covaries with its "estimated verisimilitude" (1977; forthcoming). Roughly

Some realists concede their failure to articulate a coherent notion of approximate truth or verisimilitude, but they insist that this failure in no way compromises the viability of T1. Newton-Smith, for instance, grants that "no one has given a satisfactory analysis of the notion of verisimilitude," but he insists that the concept can be legitimately invoked "even if one cannot at the time give a philosophically satisfactory analysis of it."[18] He quite rightly points out that many scientific concepts were explanatorily useful long before a philosophically coherent analysis was given for them. But the analogy is unseemly, for what is being challenged is not whether the concept of approximate truth is philosophically rigorous but, rather, whether it is even clear enough for us to ascertain whether it entails what it purportedly explains. Until someone provides a clearer analysis of approximate truth than is now available, it is not even clear whether truthlikeness would explain success, let alone whether, as Newton-Smith insists, "the concept of verisimilitude is *required* in order to give a satisfactory theoretical explanation of an aspect of the scientific enterprise."[19] The realist who would demystify the "miraculousness" (Putnam) or the "mysteriousness" (Newton-Smith)[20] of the success of science needs more than a promissory note that somehow, someday, someone will show that approximately true theories must be successful theories.[21]

---

speaking, "estimated truthlikeness" is a measure of how closely (the content of) a theory corresponds to what we take to be the best conceptual systems that we so far have been able to find (Niiniluoto, 1980, pp. 443 ff.). If Niiniluoto's measures work, it follows from the above-mentioned covariance that an empirically successful theory will have a high degree of estimated truthlikeness. But because estimated truthlikeness and genuine verisimilitude are not necessarily related (the former being parasitic on existing evidence and available conceptual systems), it is an open question whether, as Niiniluoto asserts, the continued success of highly confirmed theories can be explained by the hypothesis that they in fact are close to the truth at least in the relevant respects. Unless I am mistaken, this remark of his betrays a confusion between "true verisimilitude" (to which we have apparently no epistemic access) and "estimated verisimilitude" (which is accessible but nonepistemic).

18. Newton-Smith, forthcoming.

19. Ibid.

20. Newton-Smith claims that the increasing predictive success of science through time "would be totally mystifying . . . if it were not for the fact that theories are capturing more and more truth about the world" (forthcoming, p. 15).

21. I must stress again that I am not denying that there may be a connection between approximate truth and predictive success. I am observing only that the realists, until they show us what that connection is, should be more reticent than they are about claiming that realism can explain the success of science.

Whether there is some definition of approximate truth which does indeed entail that approximately true theories will be predictively successful (and yet still probably false) is not clear.[22] What can be said is that, promises to the contrary notwithstanding, not one of the proponents of realism has yet articulated a coherent account of approximate truth which entails that approximately true theories will, across the range where we can test them, be successful predictors. Further difficulties abound. Even if the realist had a semantically adequate characterization of approximate or partial truth, and even if that semantics entailed that most of the consequences of an approximately true theory would be true, he would still be without any criterion that would epistemically warrant the ascription of approximate truth to a theory. As it is, the realist seems to be long on intuitions and short on either a semantics or an epistemology of approximate truth.

These should be urgent items on the realists' agenda since, until we have a coherent account of what approximate truth is, central realist theses like R1, T1, and T2 are just so much mumbo jumbo.

4) *Approximate truth and success: the upward path.* — Despite the doubts voiced in section 3, let us grant for the sake of argument that if a theory is approximately true, then it will be successful. Even granting T1, is there any plausibility to the suggestion of T2 that explanatory success can be taken as a rational warrant for a judgment of approximate truth? The answer seems to be "no."

To see why, we need to explore briefly one of the connections between "genuinely referring" and being "approximately true." However the latter is understood, I take it that a realist would never want to say that a theory was approximately true if its central theoretical terms failed to refer. If there were no entities similar to atoms, no atomic theory could be approximately true; if there were no subatomic particles, no quantum theory of chemistry could be approximately true. In short, a necessary condition — especially for a scientific realist — for a theory being close to the truth is that its central explanatory terms

22. A nonrealist might argue that a theory is approximately true just in case all its observable consequences are true or within a specific interval from the true value. Theories that were "approximately true" in this sense would indeed be demonstrably successful. But, the realist's (otherwise commendable) commitment to taking seriously the theoretical claims of a theory precludes him from utilizing any such construal of approximate truth, since he wants to say that the theoretical as well as the observational consequences are approximately true.

genuinely refer. (An instrumentalist, of course, could countenance the weaker claim that a theory was approximately true just so long as its directly testable consequences were close to the observable values. But, as I argue above, the realist must take claims about approximate truth to refer alike to the observable and the deep-structural dimensions of a theory.)

Now, what the history of science offers us is a plethora of theories that were both successful and (so far as we can judge) nonreferential with respect to many of their central explanatory concepts. I have discussed earlier one specific family of theories which fits this description. Let me add a few more prominent examples to the list:

—the humoral theory of medicine;
—the effluvial theory of static electricity;
—catastrophist geology, with its commitment to a universal (Noachian) deluge;
—the phlogiston theory of chemistry;
—the caloric theory of heat;
—the vibratory theory of heat;
—the vital force theories of physiology;
—the theory of circular inertia;
—theories of spontaneous generation.

This list, which could be extended ad nauseam, involves in every instance a theory that was once successful and well confirmed, but which contained central terms that (we now believe) were nonreferring. Anyone who imagines that the theories that have been successful in the history of science have also been, with respect to their central concepts, genuinely referring theories has studied only the more whiggish versions of the history of science (i.e., the ones that recount only those past theories that are referentially similar to currently prevailing ones).

It is true that proponents of CER sometimes hedge their bets by suggesting that their analysis applies exclusively to the mature sciences (e.g., Putnam and Krajewski). This distinction between mature and immature sciences proves convenient to the realist since he can use it to dismiss any prima facie counterexample to the empirical claims of CER on the grounds that the example is drawn from an immature science. But this insulating maneuver is unsatisfactory in two respects. In the first place, it runs the risk of making CER vacuous since these authors usually define a mature science as one in which correspondence or limiting-case relations obtain invariably between any successive theories in the science once it has passed "the threshold of maturity." Krajewski grants the tautological character of this view when he notes that "the thesis that there is [correspondence] among successive theories becomes, indeed, analytical."[23] Nonetheless, he believes that there is a version of the maturity thesis which "may be and must be tested by the history of science." That version is that "every branch of science crosses at some period the threshold of maturity."[24] But the testability of this hypothesis is dubious at best. There is no historical observation that could conceivably refute it since, even if we discovered that no sciences yet possessed "corresponding" theories, it could be maintained that eventually every science will become corresponding. It is equally difficult to confirm it since, even if we found a science in which corresponding relations existed between the latest theory and its predecessor, we would have no way of knowing whether that relation will continue to apply to subsequent changes of theory in that science. In other words, the much vaunted empirical testability of realism is seriously compromised by limiting it to the mature sciences.

But there is a second unsavory dimension to the restriction of CER to the mature sciences. The realists' avowed aim, after all, is to explain why science is successful: that is the miracle they allege the nonrealists leave unaccounted for. The fact of the matter is that parts of science, including many immature sciences, have been successful for a very long time; indeed, many of the theories I allude to above were empirically successful by any criterion I can conceive of (including fertility, intuitively high confirmation, successful prediction, etc.). If the realist restricts himself to explaining only how the mature sciences work (and recall that very few sciences indeed are yet mature as the realist sees it), then he will have completely failed in his ambition to explain why science in general is successful. Moreover, several of the examples I have cited above come from the history of mathematical physics in the past century (e.g., the electromagnetic and optical aethers) and, as Putnam himself concedes, "*physics* surely counts as a 'mature' science if any science does."[25] Since realists would presumably insist that many of the central terms of the theories enumerated above do not genuinely refer, it follows that none of those theories could be approximately true

23. Krajewski, 1977, p. 91.
24. Ibid.
25. Putnam, 1978, p. 21.

(recalling that the former is a necessary condition for the latter). Accordingly, cases of this kind cast very grave doubts on the plausibility of T2, that is, the claim that nothing succeeds like approximate truth.

I daresay that for every highly successful theory in the past of science which we now believe to be a genuinely referring theory, one could find half a dozen once successful theories that we now regard as substantially nonreferring. If the proponents of CER are the empiricists they profess to be about matters epistemological, cases of this kind and this frequency should give them pause about the well-foundedness of T2.

But we need not limit our counterexamples to nonreferring theories. Many theories in the past, so far as we can tell, were both genuinely referring and empirically successful, but we are nonetheless loathe to regard them as approximately true. Consider, for instance, virtually all those geological theories prior to the 1960s which denied any lateral motion to the continents. Such theories were, by any standard, highly successful (and apparently referential); but would anyone today be prepared to say that their constituent theoretical claims—committed as they were to laterally stable continents—are almost true? Is it not the fact of the matter that structural geology was a successful science between (say) 1920 and 1960, even though geologists were fundamentally mistaken about many, perhaps even most, of the basic mechanisms of tectonic construction? Or what about the chemical theories of the 1920s which assumed that the atomic nucleus was structurally homogenous? Or those chemical and physical theories of the late nineteenth century which explicitly assumed that matter was neither created nor destroyed? I am aware of no sense of approximate truth (available to the realist) according to which such highly successful, but evidently false, theoretical assumptions could be regarded as truthlike.

More generally, the realist needs a riposte to the prima facie plausible claim that there is no necessary connection between increasing the accuracy of our deep-structural characterizations of nature and improvements at the level of phenomenological explanations, predictions, and manipulations. It seems entirely conceivable intuitively that the theoretical mechanisms of a new theory, T_n, might be closer to the mark than those of a rival T_o, and yet T_o might be more accurate at the level of testable predictions. In the absence of an argument that closer correspondence at the level of unobservable claims is more likely than not to reveal itself in greater accuracy at the experimental level, one is obliged to say that the realist's hunch that increasing deep-structural fidelity must manifest itself pragmatically in the form of heightened experimental accuracy has yet to be made cogent. (Equally problematic, of course, is the inverse argument to the effect that increasing experimental accuracy betokens greater truthlikeness at the level of theoretical, i.e., deep-structural, commitments.)

5) *Confusions about convergence and retention.* — Thus far I have discussed only the static or synchronic versions of CER, versions that make absolute rather than relative judgments about truthlikeness. Of equal appeal have been those variants of CER which invoke a notion of what is variously called convergence, correspondence, or cumulation. Proponents of the diachronic version of CER supplement the arguments discussed above (S1-S4 and T1-T2) with an additional set. They tend to be of this form:

C1) If earlier theories in a scientific domain are successful and thereby, according to realist principles (e.g., S3 above), approximately true, then scientists should accept only later theories that retain appropriate portions of earlier theories.

C2) As a matter of fact, scientists do adopt the strategy of C1 and manage to produce new, more successful, theories in the process.

C3) The fact that scientists succeed at retaining appropriate parts of earlier theories in more successful successors shows that the earlier theories did genuinely refer and that they were approximately true. And thus, the strategy propounded in C1 is sound.[26]

Perhaps the prevailing view here is Putnam's and (implicitly) Popper's, according to which rationally warranted successor theories in a mature science must (*a*) contain reference to the entities apparently referred to in the predecessor theory (since, by hypothesis, the terms in the earlier theory refer), and (*b*) contain the "theoretical laws" and "mechanisms" of the predecessor theory as limiting cases. As Putnam tells us, a realist should insist that any viable successor to a theory T_0 must "contain the laws of T_0 as a limiting case."[27] John Watkins, a

26. If this argument, which I attribute to the realists, seems a bit murky, I challenge any reader to find a more clear-cut one in the literature. Overt formulations of this position may be found in Putnam, Boyd, and Newton-Smith.

27. Putnam, 1978, p. 21.

like-minded convergentist, puts the point this way: "It typically happens in the history of science that when some hitherto dominant theory T is superceded by T', T' is in the relation of correspondence to T [i.e., T is a limiting case of T']."[28]

Numerous recent philosophers of science have subscribed to a similar view, including Popper, Post, Krajewski, and Koertge.[29] This form of retention is not the only one to have been widely discussed. Indeed, realists have espoused a wide variety of claims about what is or should be retained in the transition from a once successful predecessor (T_0) to a successor (T_n) theory. Among the more important forms of realist retention are the following: (1) T_n entails T_0 (Whewell); (2) T_n retains the true consequences or truth content of T_0 (Popper); (3) T_n retains the "confirmed" portions of T_0 (Post, Koertge); (4) T_n preserves the "theoretical laws and mechanisms" of T_0 (Boyd, McMullin, Putnam); (5) T_n preserves T_0 as a limiting case (Watkins, Putnam, Krajewski); (6) T_n explains why T_0 succeeded insofar as T_0 succeeded (Sellars); (7) T_n retains reference for the central terms of T_0 (Putnam, Boyd). The question before us is whether, when retention is understood in any of these senses, the realist's theses about convergence and retention are correct.

5.1) *Do scientists adopt the retentionist strategy of CER?* — One part of the convergent realist's argument is a claim to the effect that scientists generally adopt the strategy of seeking to preserve earlier theories in later ones. As Putnam puts it, "preserving the *mechanisms* of the earlier theory as often as possible, which is what scientists try to do. . . . That scientists try to do this . . . is a fact, and that this strategy has led to important discoveries . . . is also a fact."[30] In a similar vein, Szumi-

28. Watkins, 1978, pp. 376-377.

29. Popper (1959, p. 276) writes: "a theory which has been well corroborated can only be superseded by one . . . [which] *contains* the old well-corroborated theory—or at least a good approximation to it." Post (1971, p. 229) says: "I shall even claim that, as a matter of empirical historical fact, [successor] theories [have] always explained the *whole* of [the well-confirmed part of their predecessors]." And Koertge (1973, pp. 176-177) writes: "nearly all pairs of successive theories in the history of science stand in a correspondence relation and . . . where there is no correspondence to begin with, the new theory will be developed in such a way that it comes more nearly into correspondence with the old." Among other authors who have defended a similar view, one should mention Fine (1967), Kordig (1971), Margenau (1950), and Sklar (1967).

30. Putnam, 1978, p. 20. Putnam fails to point out that it is also a fact that many scientists do not seek to preserve earlier mechanisms and that theories that have not preserved earlier theoretical mechanisms (whether the germ theory of disease, plate tectonics, or wave optics) have led to important discoveries.

lewicz (although not stressing realism) insists that many eminent scientists made it a main heuristic requirement of their research programs that a new theory stand in a relation of correspondence with the theory it supersedes.[31] If Putnam and the other retentionists are right about the cognitive goals that most scientists have adopted, we should expect to find the historical literature of science abundantly provided with (*a*) proofs that later theories do indeed contain earlier theories as limiting cases, or (*b*) outright rejections of later theories that fail to contain earlier theories. Except on rare occasions (coming primarily from the history of mechanics), one finds neither of these concerns prominent in the literature of science. For instance, to the best of my knowledge, literally no one criticized the wave theory of light because it did not preserve the theoretical mechanisms of the earlier corpuscular theory; no one faulted Lyell's uniformitarian geology on the grounds that it dispensed with several causal processes prominent in catastrophist geology; Darwin's theory was not criticized by most geologists for its failure to retain many of the mechanisms of Lamarckian evolutionary theory.

For all the realist's confident claims about the prevalence of a retentionist value in the sciences, I am aware of no historical studies that would sustain as a general thesis his hypothesis about the evaluative strategies utilized in science. Moreover, insofar as Putnam and Boyd claim to be offering "an explanation of the [retentionist] behavior of scientists,"[32] they have the wrong explanandum, for, if there is any widespread strategy in science, it is one that says, "accept an empirically successful theory, regardless of whether it contains the theoretical laws and mechanisms of its predecessors."[33] Indeed, one could take a leaf from the realist's C2 and claim that the success of the strategy of assuming that earlier theories do not generally refer shows that it is true that earlier theories generally do not.

(One might note in passing how often, and on what evidence, realists imagine that they are speaking for the scientific majority. Putnam, for instance, claims that "realism is, so to speak, 'science's philosophy of science,'" and that "science taken at 'face value' *implies* realism."[34]

31. Szumilewicz, 1977.
32. Putnam, 1978, p. 21.
33. I have written a book about this strategy (Laudan, 1977).
34. After the epistemological and methodological battles about science during the past three hundred years, it should be fairly clear that science, taken at its face value, implies no particular epistemology.

Hooker insists that to be a realist is to take science "seriously,"[35] as if to suggest that conventionalists, instrumentalists, and positivists such as Duhem, Poincaré, and Mach did not take science seriously. The willingness of some realists to attribute realist motives to working scientists — on the strength of virtually no empirical research into the values that in fact have guided scientific practice — raises doubts about the seriousness of their commitment to the empirical character of epistemic claims.)

5.2) *Do later theories preserve the mechanisms, models, and laws of earlier theories?* — Regardless of the explicit strategies to which scientists have subscribed, are Putnam and several other retentionists right that later theories typically entail earlier theories, and that "earlier theories are, very often, limiting cases of later theories"?[36] Unfortunately, answering this question is difficult, since "typically" is one of those weasel words which allows for much hedging. I shall assume that Putnam and Watkins mean that "most of the time (or perhaps in most of the important cases) successor theories contain predecessor theories as limiting cases." So construed, the claim is patently false. Copernican astronomy did not retain all the key mechanisms of Ptolemaic astronomy and optics; Franklin's electrical theory did not contain its predecessor (Nollet's) as a limiting case. Relativistic physics did not retain the aether or the mechanisms associated with it; statistical mechanics does not incorporate all the mechanisms of thermodynamics; modern genetics does not have Darwinian pangenesis as a limiting case; the wave theory of light did not appropriate the mechanisms of corpuscular optics; modern embryology incorporates few of the mechanisms prominent in classical embryological theory. As I have shown elsewhere,[37] loss occurs at virtually every level: the confirmed predictions of earlier theories are sometimes not explained by later ones; even the observable laws explained by earlier theories are not always retained, not even as limiting cases; the theoretical mechanisms of earlier theories are, as frequently as not, treated as flotsam. The point is that some of the most important theoretical innovations have been due to a willingness of scientists to violate the cumulationist or retentionist constraints which realists enjoin mature scientists to follow.

35. Hooker, 1974, pp. 467-472.
36. Putnam, 1978, pp. 20, 123.
37. Laudan, 1976.

There is a deep reason why the convergent realist is wrong about these matters. It has to do, in part, with the role of ontological frameworks in science and with the nature of so-called limiting-case relations. As scientists use the term "limiting case," T_0 can be a limiting case of T_n only if (*a*) all the variables (observable and theoretical) assigned a value in T_0 are assigned a value by T_n and (*b*) the values assigned to every variable of T_n are the same as, or very close to, the values T_0 assigns to the corresponding variable when certain initial and boundary conditions—consistent with T_n—are specified.[38] This seems to require that T_0 can be a limiting case of T_n only if all the entities postulated by T_0 occur in the ontology of T_n. Whenever there is a change of ontology accompanying a theory transition such that T_n (when conjoined with suitable initial and boundary conditions) fails to capture T_0's ontology, then T_0 cannot be a limiting case of T_n. Even when the ontologies of T_n and T_0 overlap appropriately (i.e., when T_n's ontology embraces all T_0's), T_0 is a limiting case of T_n only if all the laws of T_0 can be derived from T_n, given appropriate limiting conditions. It is important to stress that both these conditions (among others) must be satisfied before one theory can be a limiting case of another. Whereas "closet positivists" might be content with capturing only the formal mathematical relations or only the observable consequences of T_0 within a successor, T_n, any genuine realist must insist that T_0's underlying ontology is preserved in T_n's, for it is that ontology above all which he alleges to be approximately true.

Too often, philosophers (and physicists) infer the existence of a limiting-case relation between T_n and T_0 on substantially less than this. For instance, many writers have claimed one theory to be a limiting case of another when only some, but not all, of the laws of the former are derivable from the latter. In other instances, one theory has been

38. This matter of limiting conditions consistent with the "reducing" theory is curious. Some of the best-known expositions of limiting-case relations depend (as Krajewski has observed) upon showing an earlier theory to be a limiting case of a later theory only by adopting limiting assumptions explicitly denied by the later theory. For instance, several standard textbook discussions present (a portion of) classical mechanics as a limiting case of special relativity, provided c approaches infinity. But special relativity is committed to the claim that c is a constant. Is there not something suspicious about a derivation of one theory from another which essentially involves an assumption inconsistent with the deriving theory? If the deriving theory is correct, then it specifically denies the adoption of a premise commonly used to prove the derived theory as a limiting case. (It should be noted that most such proofs can be reformulated unobjectionably, e.g., in the relativity case, by letting $v \rightarrow 0$ rather than $c \rightarrow \infty$.)

said to be a limiting case of a successor when the mathematical laws of the former find homologies in the latter, but when the former's ontology is not fully extractable from the latter's.

Consider one prominent example which has often been misdescribed, namely, the transition from the classical aether theory to relativistic and quantum mechanics. It can, of course, be shown that some laws of classical mechanics are limiting cases of relativistic mechanics. But there are other laws and general assertions made by the classical theory (e.g., claims about the density and fine structure of the aether, general laws about the character of the interaction between aether and matter, models and mechanisms detailing the compressibility of the aether) which could not conceivably be limiting cases of modern mechanics. The reason is a simple one: a theory cannot assign values to a variable that does not occur in that theory's language (or, more colloquially, it cannot assign properties to entities whose existence it does not countenance). Classical aether physics contained a number of postulated mechanisms for dealing, inter alia, with the transmission of light through the aether. Such mechanisms could not possibly appear in a successor theory like the special theory of relativity, which denies the very existence of an aetherial medium and which accomplishes the explanatory tasks performed by the aether via very different mechanisms.

Nineteenth-century mathematical physics is replete with similar examples of evidently successful mathematical theories which, because some of their variables refer to entities whose existence we now deny, cannot be shown to be limiting cases of our physics. As Adolf Grünbaum has cogently argued, when we are confronted with two incompatible theories, T_n and T_0, such that T_n does not contain all of T_0's ontology, then the mechanisms and theoretical laws of T_0 which involve the entities not postulated by T_n cannot possibly be retained — not even as limiting cases — in T_n.[39] This result is of some significance. What little plausibility convergent or retentive realism has enjoyed derives from the presumption that it correctly describes the relationship between classical and postclassical mechanics and gravitational theory. Once we see that even in this prima facie most favorable case for the realist (where some of the laws of the predecessor theory are genuinely limiting cases of the successor), changing ontologies or con-

---

39. Grünbaum, 1976.

ceptual frameworks make it impossible to capture many of the central theoretical laws and mechanisms postulated by the earlier theory, then we can see how misleading is Putnam's claim that "what scientists try to do" is to preserve

> the *mechanisms* of the earlier theory as often as possible—or to show
> that they are 'limiting cases' of new mechanisms. . . . [40]

Where the mechanisms of the earlier theory involve entities whose existence the later theory denies, no scientist does (or should) feel any compunction about wholesale repudiation of the earlier mechanisms.

But even where there is no change in basic ontology, many theories (even in "mature sciences" like physics) fail to retain all the explanatory successes of their predecessors. It is well known, for instance, that statistical mechanics has yet to capture the irreversibility of macro-thermodynamics as a genuine limiting case. Classical continuum mechanics has not yet been reduced to quantum mechanics or relativity. Contemporary field theory has yet to replicate the classical thesis that physical laws are invariant under reflection in space. If scientists had taken seriously the realist's demand that new theories must have old theories as limiting cases, neither relativity nor statistical mechanics could have been accepted as viable theories. It has been said before, but it needs to be reiterated over and again: *a proof of the existence of limiting relations between selected components of two theories is a far cry from a systematic proof that one theory* is a *limiting case of the other.* Even if classical and modern physics did stand to one another in the manner in which the convergent realist erroneously imagines they do, his hasty generalization that theory successions in all the advanced sciences show limiting case relations is patently false.[41] But, as this discussion shows, not even the realist's paradigm case will sustain the claims he is apt to make about it.

What this analysis underscores is just how reactionary many forms of convergent epistemological realism are. If one took seriously CER's advice to reject any new theory that did not capture existing (mature)

---

40. Putnam, 1978, p. 20.
41. As Mario Bunge has cogently put it (1970, pp. 309-310): "The popular view on inter-theory relations . . . that every new theory includes (as regards its extension) its predecessors . . . is philosophically superficial, . . . and it is false as a historical hypothesis concerning the advancement of science."

theories as referential and existing laws and mechanisms as approximately authentic, then any prospect for deep-structure, ontological changes in our theories would be foreclosed. Equally outlawed would be any significant repudiation of present-day theoretical models. Thus, despite his commitment to the growth of knowledge, the realist would unwittingly freeze science in its present state by forcing all future theories to accommodate the ontology of contemporary (mature) science and by foreclosing the possibility that future generations may come to the conclusion that some (or even most) of the central terms in our best-tested theories are no more referential than was "natural place," "phlogiston," "aether," or "caloric."

5.3) *Could theories converge in ways required by the realist?* — These instances of violations of the sorts of continuity usually required by realists are by themselves sufficient to show that the form of scientific growth which the convergent realist takes as his explicandum is often absent, even in the mature sciences. But we can move beyond this handful of specific cases to show in principle that the kind of cumulation demanded by the realist is unattainable. Specifically, by drawing on some results established by David Miller and others, the following can be shown:

   a) the familiar requirement that a successor theory, T_n, must both preserve as true the true consequences of its predecessor, T_0, and explain T_0's anomalies is contradictory;

   b) that if a T_n involves a change in the ontology or conceptual framework of a predecessor, T_0, then T_0 will have true and determinate consequences not possessed by T_n;

   c) that if two theories, T_n and T_0, disagree, each will have true and determinate consequences not exhibited by the other.

In order to establish these conclusions, one needs to utilize a "syntactic" view of theories according to which a theory is a conjunction of statements and its consequences are defined a la Tarski in terms of content classes. Needless to say, this is neither the only nor necessarily the best way of thinking about theories; but it happens to be the way in which most philosophers who argue for convergence and retention (e.g., Popper, Watkins, Post, Krajewski, and Niiniluoto) tend to conceive of theories. If, as they do, one utilizes the Tarskian conception of a theory's content and its consequences, then the familiar convergentist theses alluded to in (*a*) through (*c*) make no sense.

The elementary but devastating consequences of Miller's analysis establish that virtually any effort to link scientific progress or growth to the wholesale retention of a predecessor theory's Tarskian content or logical consequences or true consequences or observed consequences or confirmed consequences is evidently doomed. Realists have not only got their history wrong insofar as they imagine that cumulative retention has prevailed in science, but we can see that, given their views on what should be retained through theory change, history could not possibly have been the way their models require it to be. In short, the realists' strictures on cumulativity are as ill-advised normatively as they are false historically.

Along with many other realists, Putnam has claimed that "the mature sciences do converge . . . and that that convergence has great explanatory value for the theory of science."[42] As this section should show, Putnam and his fellow realists are arguably wrong on both counts. Popper once remarked that "no theory of knowledge should attempt to explain why we are successful in our attempts to explain things."[43] Such a dogma is too strong. But what the foregoing analysis shows is that an occupational hazard of recent epistemology is imagining that convincing explanations of our success come easily or cheaply.

6) *Should new theories explain why their predecessors were successful?* — An apparently more modest realism than that outlined above is familiar in the form of the requirement (R4) often attributed to Sellars: that every satisfactory new theory must be able to explain why its predecessor was successful insofar as it was successful. In this view, viable new theories need not preserve all the content of their predecessors or capture those predecessors as limiting cases. Rather, it is simply insisted that a viable new theory, T_n, must explain why, when we conceive of the world according to the old theory, T_o, there is a range of cases where our T_o-guided expectations were correct or approximately correct, even though T_o is (held to be) false.

What are we to make of this requirement? In the first place, it is clearly gratuitous. If T_n has more confirmed consequences (and more conceptual simplicity) than T_o, then T_n is preferable to T_o even if T_n cannot explain why T_o was successful. Contrariwise, if T_n has fewer confirmed consequences than T_o, then T_n cannot be rationally preferred to T_o even if T_n does manage to explain why T_o was successful.

42. Putnam, 1978, p. 37.
43. Popper, 1963, p. 23.

In short, a theory's ability to explain why a rival is successful is neither a necessary nor a sufficient condition for judging it to be better than its rival.

Other difficulties likewise confront the claim that new theories should explain why their predecessors were successful. Chief among them is the ambiguity of the notion of "explaining why a predecessor theory was successful." One way to explain why T_0 was successful is to show that it shares many confirmed consequences with a highly successful T_n. But this is not an explanation that a scientific realist could accept, since it makes no reference to, and thus does not depend upon, an epistemic assessment of either T_0 or T_n. (After all, an instrumentalist could quite happily grant that if T_n is a pragmatically successful theory, then insofar as T_0 and T_n have overlapping or experimentally indistinguishable consequences, T_0 should also succeed at "saving the phenomena.")

The intuition being traded on in this persuasive Sellarsian account is that the pragmatic success of a new theory, combined with a partial comparison of the respective consequences of the new theory and its predecessor, will sometimes put us in a position to say when the older theory worked and when it failed. But such comparisons as can be made in this manner do not involve epistemic appraisals of either the new or the old theory qua theories. Accordingly, the possibility of such comparisons and of such explanations provides no specific argument for epistemic realism, since the nonrealist tells (and with a much clearer conscience) precisely the same pragmatic story about success.

What the realist apparently needs here is an epistemically robust sense of explaining the success of a predecessor. Such an epistemic characterization would presumably begin with the claim that T_n was approximately true and would proceed to show that the observable claims of its predecessor, T_0, deviated only slightly from (some of) the observable consequences of T_n. It would then be alleged that the (presumed) approximate truth of T_n and the partly overlapping consequences of T_0 and T_n jointly explained why T_0 was successful insofar as it was successful. But this is a non sequitur. As I have shown above, the fact that T_n is approximately true does not even explain why T_n is successful; how, under those circumstances, can the approximate truth of T_n explain why some theory different from T_n is successful? Whatever the nature of the relations between T_n and T_0 (entailment, limiting case, etc.), the epistemic ascription of approximate truth to either T_n or T_o (or both) apparently leaves untouched questions of how successful T_n and T_o are.

7) *The realists' ultimate petitio principii.* — It is time to step back a moment from the details of the realists' argument to look at its general strategy. Fundamentally, the realist is utilizing, as we have seen, an abductive inference that proceeds from the success of science to the conclusion that science is approximately true, verisimilar, or referential (or any combination of these). This argument, commonly known as "inference to the best explanation," is meant to show the skeptic that theories are not ill gotten, the positivist that theories are not reducible to their observational consequences, and the pragmatist that classical epistemic categories (e.g., truth, falsity) are a relevant part of metascientific discourse.

It is little short of remarkable that realists would imagine that their critics would find the argument compelling. As I have shown elsewhere,[44] ever since antiquity critics of epistemic realism have based their skepticism upon a deep-rooted conviction that the fallacy of affirming the consequent is indeed fallacious. When Sextus or Bellarmine or Hume doubted that certain theories which saved the phenomena were warrantable as true, their doubts were based on a belief that the exhibition that a theory had some true consequences left entirely open the truth status of the theory. Indeed, many nonrealists have been nonrealists precisely because they believed that false theories, as well as true ones, could have true consequences.

Now enters the new breed of realist (e.g., Putnam, Boyd, Newton-Smith) who wants to argue that epistemic realism can reasonably be presumed to be true by virtue of the fact that it has true consequences. But this is a monumental case of begging the question. The nonrealist refuses to admit that a scientific theory can be warrantedly judged to be true simply because it has some true consequences. Such nonrealists are not likely to be impressed by the claim that a philosophical theory like realism can be warranted as true because it arguably has some true consequences. If nonrealists are chary about first-order abductions to avowedly true conclusions, they are not likely to be impressed by second-order abductions, particularly when, as I have tried to show above, the premises and conclusions are so indeterminate.

But, it might be argued, the realist is not out to convert the intransi-

44. Laudan, 1978.

gent skeptic or the determined instrumentalist.[45] He is perhaps seeking, rather, to show that realism can be tested like any other scientific hypothesis, and that realism is at least as well confirmed as some of our best scientific theories. Such an analysis, however plausible initially, will not stand up to scrutiny. I am aware of no realist who is willing to say that a scientific theory can be reasonably presumed to be true or even regarded as well confirmed just on the strength of the fact that its thus far tested consequences are true. Realists have long been in the forefront of those opposed to ad hoc and post hoc theories. Before a realist accepts a scientific hypothesis, he wants to know whether it has explained or predicted more than it was devised to explain; he wants to know whether it has been subjected to a battery of controlled tests, whether it has successfully made novel predictions, whether there is independent evidence for it.

What, then, of realism itself as a scientific hypothesis?[46] Even if we grant (contrary to what I argue in chap. 3) that realism entails and thus explains the success of science, ought that (hypothetical) success warrant, by the realist's own construal of scientific acceptability, the acceptance of realism? Since this form of realism was devised in order to explain the success of science, it remains purely ad hoc with respect to that success. If realism has made some novel predictions or been subjected to carefully controlled tests, one does not learn about it from the literature of contemporary realism. At the risk of apparent inconsistency, the realist repudiates the instrumentalist's view that merely "saving the phenomena" is a significant form of evidential support, while endorsing realism itself on the transparently instrumentalist grounds that it is confirmed by those very facts it was invented to

45. I owe the suggestion of this realist response to Andrew Lugg.

46. I find Putnam's views on the empirical or scientific character of realism rather perplexing. At some points he seems to suggest that realism is both empirical and scientific. Thus, he writes: "If realism is an explanation of this fact [namely, that science is successful], realism must itself be an over-arching scientific *hypothesis*" (1978, p. 19). Since Putnam clearly maintains the antecedent, he seems committed to the consequent. Elsewhere he refers to certain realist tenets as being "our highest level empirical generalizations about knowledge" (p. 37). He says moreover that realism "could be false," and that "facts are relevant to its support (or to criticize it)" (pp. 78-79). Nonetheless, for reasons he has not made clear, Putnam wants to deny that realism is either scientific or a hypothesis (p. 79). How realism can consist of doctrines which (1) explain facts about the world, (2) are empirical generalizations about knowledge, and (3) can be confirmed or falsified by evidence and yet be neither scientific nor hypothetical is left opaque.

explain. No proponent of realism has sought to show that realism satisfies those stringent empirical demands that the realist himself minimally insists on when appraising scientific theories. The latter-day
realist often calls realism a "scientific" or "well-tested" hypothesis but
seems curiously reluctant to subject it to those controls he otherwise
takes to be a sine qua non for empirical well-foundedness.

8) *Conclusion.* — The arguments and cases discussed above seem to
warrant the following conclusions:

1. The fact that a theory's central terms refer does not entail that it
will be successful, and a theory's success is no warrant for the claim
that all or most of its central terms refer.

2. The notion of approximate truth is presently too vague to permit
one to judge whether a theory consisting entirely of approximately true
laws would be empirically successful. What is clear is that a theory may
be empirically successful even if it is not approximately true. "Inference to the best explanation" is just a form of epistemic sleight of hand.

3. Realists have no explanation whatever for the fact that many theories that are not approximately true and whose theoretical terms
seemingly do not refer are nonetheless often successful.

4. The convergentist's assertion that scientists in a mature discipline
usually preserve, or seek to preserve, the laws and mechanisms of earlier theories in later ones has not been established and is probably
false; his assertion that, when such laws are preserved in a successful
successor, we can explain the success of the former by virtue of the
truthlikeness of the preserved laws and mechanisms, suffers from all
the defects noted above confronting approximate truth.

5. Even if it could be shown that referring theories and approximately true theories would be successful, the realists' argument that
successful theories are approximately true and genuinely referential
takes for granted precisely what the nonrealist denies: namely, that
explanatory success betokens truth.

6. It is not clear that acceptable theories either do or should explain
why their predecessors succeeded or failed. If a theory is better supported than its rivals and predecessors, then it is not epistemically
decisive whether it explains why its rivals worked.

7. If a theory has once been falsified, it is unreasonable to expect
that a successor should retain either all of its content or its confirmed
consequences or its theoretical mechanisms.

8. Nowhere has the realist established — except by fiat — that non-

realist epistemologists lack the resources to explain the success of science.

With these specific conclusions in mind, we can proceed to a more global one. It is not yet established—Putnam, Newton-Smith, and Boyd notwithstanding—that realism can explain any part of the success of science. What is very clear is that realism cannot, even by its own lights, explain the success of those many theories whose central terms have evidently not referred and whose theoretical laws and mechanisms were not approximately true. The inescapable conclusion is that, insofar as many realists are concerned with explaining how science works and with assessing the adequacy of their epistemology by that standard, they have thus far failed to explain very much. Their epistemology and axiology are confronted by anomalies which seem beyond their resources to grapple with.

To put it specifically in the language of earlier chapters of this essay, the realist offers us a set of aims for science with these features: (1) we do not know how to achieve them (since there is no methodology for warranting the truthlikeness of universal claims); (2) we could not recognize ourselves as having achieved those aims even if, mysteriously, we had managed to achieve them (since the realist offers no epistemic, as opposed to semantic, tokens of truthlikeness); (3) we cannot even tell whether we are moving closer to achieving them (since we generally cannot tell for any two theories which one is closer to the truth); and (4) many of the most successful theories in the history of science (e.g., aether theories) have failed to exemplify them. In my view, any one of these failings would be sufficient to raise grave doubts about the realist's proposed axiology and methodology for science. Taken together, they seem to constitute as damning an indictment of a set of cognitive values as we find anywhere in the historical record. Major epistemologies of the past (e.g., classical empiricism, inductivism, instrumentalism, pragmatism, infallibilism, positivism) have been abandoned on grounds far flimsier than these.

EPILOGUE

Readers who have followed the argument this far may well be expecting me finally to deliver the goods by stating what the central values, aims, and methods of science are, or at least what they should be. Any such expectations will, I am afraid, be dashed. To lay out a set of cognitive aims and methods and to say "those are what science is about" would be to undermine much of the foregoing analysis, for we have seen time and again that the aims of science vary, and quite appropriately so, from one epoch to another, from one scientific field to another, and sometimes among researchers in the same field. We have also seen that, even among researchers who share the same aims or values, methods may legitimately differ.

What I do claim to have exhibited here is some of the analytic machinery we can bring to bear in assessing proposed aims and methods. More than that, I have shown by example how that machinery can be applied to the critique of some popular and initially plausible, but ultimately unsatisfactory, axiologies of science (e.g., scientific realism and epistemic relativism).

One is tempted to speculate whether the model of methodological and axiological critique sketched out here could be adapted to deal with extrascientific axiologies, such as those of moral theory. For my part, I have resisted the temptation to draw out several of the apparent parallels between debates about cognitive values and debates about moral or political values. The reason is straightforward: one fights one battle at a time. If the analysis of cognitive values developed here should stand up to the criticisms it will probably provoke, then one might explore its applicability to various noncognitive axiologies. But, until we are clear about the dynamics of cognitive value change, I think it would be premature to try to work our way through the mechanics of moral axiological debate, for the latter appears to be significantly more complex. And if my colleagues in moral philosophy will forgive me for saying so, the axiological problems of meta-epistemology must be clarified before we can hope to make much headway in meta-ethics. After all, the epistemic claim of the moralist to know what he is about takes for granted a prior clarification of the aim-theoretic structure of knowledge.

REFERENCES

Barber, Bernard (1961). "Resistance by Scientists to Scientific Discovery," *Science* 134:596 ff.

Barnes, Barry (1982). *T. S. Kuhn and Social Science*. New York: Columbia University Press.

Boyd, Richard (1973). "Realism, Underdetermination, and a Causal Theory of Evidence," *Nous* 7:1-12.

Bunge, Mario (1970). "Problems Concerning Intertheory Relations." *In* P. Weingartner and G. Zecha, eds., *Induction, Physics and Ethics*. Dordrecht: Reidel. Pp. 285-315.

Campbell, N. R. (1952). *What Is Science?* New York: Dover.

——— (1957). *Foundations of Science*. New York: Dover.

Collins, Harry (1981*a*). "Son of Seven Sexes," *Social Studies of Science* 11: 33-62.

——— (1981*b*). "Stages in the Empirical Programme of Relativism," *Social Studies of Science* 11:3-10.

Dewey, John (1938). *Logic, The Theory of Inquiry*. New York: Holt.

Doppelt, Gerald (1978). "Kuhn's Epistemological Relativism: An Interpretation and Defense," *Inquiry* 21:33-86.

Feyerabend, Paul (1978). *Against Method*. New York: Schocken.

Fine, Arthur (1967). "Consistency, Derivability and Scientific Change," *Journal of Philosophy* 64:231 ff.

Grünbaum, Adolf (1976). "Can a Theory Answer More Questions than One of Its Rivals?" *British Journal for Philosophy of Science* 27:1-23.

Gutting, Gary (1973). "Conceptual Structures and Scientific Change," *Studies in History and Philosophy of Science* 4:227 ff.

Gutting, Gary, ed. (1980). *Paradigms and Revolutions*. Notre Dame: University of Notre Dame Press.

Hartley, David (1749). *Observations on Man*. London.

Hooker, Clifford (1974). "Systematic Realism," *Synthese* 26:409-497.

Hull, David, et al. (1978). "Planck's Principle," *Science* 202:717-723.

Koertge, Noretta (1973). "Theory Change in Science." *In* G. Pearce and P. Maynard, eds., *Conceptual Change*. Dordrecht: Reidel. Pp. 167-198.

Kordig, Carl (1971). "Scientific Transitions, Meaning Invariance, and Derivability," *Southern Journal of Philosophy* 1:119-125.

Krajewski, W. (1977). *Correspondence Principle and Growth of Science*. Dordrecht: Reidel.

Kuhn, Thomas (1962). *The Structure of Scientific Revolutions*. Chicago: University of Chicago Press.

———— (1970). "Reflections on My Critics." *In* I. Lakatos and A. Musgrave, *Criticism and the Growth of Knowledge*. Cambridge: Cambridge University Press.

———— (1977). *The Essential Tension*. Chicago: University of Chicago Press.

Lakatos, Imre (1978). *The Methodology of Scientific Research Programmes*. Cambridge: Cambridge University Press.

Laudan, Larry (1968). "Theories of Scientific Method from Plato to Mach," *History of Science* 7:1-63.

———— (1976). "Two Dogmas of Methodology," *Philosophy of Science* 43: 467-472.

———— (1977). *Progress and Its Problems*. Berkeley, Los Angeles, London: University of California Press.

———— (1978). "Ex-Huming Hacking," *Erkenntnis* 13:417-435.

———— (1981). *Science and Hypothesis*. Dordrecht: Reidel.

———— (1982). "The Demise of Demarcation." *In* R. S. Cohen and L. Laudan, eds., *Physics, Philosophy and Psychiatry*. Dordrecht: Reidel. Pp. 111-128.

———— (forthcoming). *Science and Method*.

Lugg, Andrew (1978). "Disagreement in Science," *Zeitschrift für allgemeine Wissenschaftstheorie* 9:276-292.

McMullin, Ernan (1970). "The History and Philosophy of Science: A Taxonomy." *In* R. Stuewer, ed., *Minnesota Studies in the Philosophy of Science* V:12-67. Minneapolis: University of Minnesota Press.

Margenau, Henry (1950). *The Nature of Physical Reality*. New York: McGraw-Hill.

Merton, Robert (1968). *Social Theory and Social Structure*. New York: Free Press.

———— (1973). *Sociology of Science*. Chicago: University of Chicago Press.

Mitroff, Ian (1974). *The Subjective Side of Science*. New York: Elsevier.

Mulkay, Michael (1977). "Sociology of the Scientific Research Community." *In* I. Spiegel-Rosing and D. Price, eds., *Science, Technology and Society.* Beverly Hills: Sage.

Musgrave, Alan (1980). "Kuhn's Second Thoughts." *In* Gutting, 1980.

Nagel, Ernest (1961). *The Structure of Science.* New York: Harcourt Brace.

Newton-Smith, William (1978). "The Underdetermination of Theories by Data," *Proceedings of the Aristotelian Society.* Pp. 71-91.

—— (forthcoming). "In Defense of Truth."

Niiniluoto, Ilkka (1977). "On the Truthlikeness of Generalizations." *In* R. Butts and J. Hintikka, eds., *Basic Problems in Methodology and Linguistics.* Dordrecht: Reidel. Pp. 121-147.

—— (1980). "Scientific Progress," *Synthese* 45:427-462.

Planck, Max (1949). *Scientific Autobiography.* New York: Philosophical Library.

Polanyi, Michael (1951). *The Logic of Liberty.* Chicago: University of Chicago Press.

Popper, Karl (1959). *Logic of Scientific Discovery.* New York: Basic Books.

—— (1963). *Conjectures and Refutations.* London: Routledge & Kegan Paul.

—— (1972). *Objective Knowledge.* Oxford: Oxford University Press.

Post, Heinz (1971). "Correspondence, Invariance and Heuristics: In Praise of Conservative Induction," *Studies in History and Philosophy of Science* 2: 213-255.

Prevost, Pierre (1804). *Essais de Philosophie.* Paris.

Prevost, Pierre, ed. (1805). *Notice de la Vie de des Écrits de George-Louis Lesage.* Geneva.

Price, Derek (1959). "Contra-Copernicus." *In* M. Clagett, ed. *Critical Problems in the History of Science.* Madison: University of Wisconsin Press. Pp. 197-218.

Putnam, Hilary (1975). *Mathematics, Matter and Method.* Vol. 1. Cambridge: Cambridge University Press.

—— (1978). *Meaning and the Moral Sciences.* London: Routledge & Kegan Paul.

Reichenbach, Hans (1938). *Experience and Prediction.* Chicago: University of Chicago Press.

Sellars, Wilfrid (1963). *Science, Perception and Reality.* New York: Humanities Press.

Sklar, Lawrence (1967). "Types of Inter-Theoretic Reductions," *British Journal for Philosophy of Science* 18:190-224.

Stewart, Dugald (1854-). *Selected Works.* Ed. W. Hamilton. Edinburgh.

Szumilewicz, I. (1977). "Incommensurability and the Rationality of the Development of Science," *British Journal for Philosophy of Science* 28:348.

Watkins, John (1978). "Corroboration and the Problem of Content-Comparison." *In* G. Radnitzky and A. Andersson, eds., *Progress and Rationality in Science*. Dordrecht: Reidel. Pp. 339-378.

Whewell, William (1851). "Of the Transformation of Hypotheses in the History of Science," *Transactions of the Cambridge Philosophical Society* 9: 139-147.

Ziman, John (1968). *Public Knowledge*. New York: Cambridge University Press.

INDEX

Aether theories, 57, 113-114, 129
Agreement and difference, 81, 94
Analogy, 58, 59
Aristotle, 31-32
Atomism, 7, 13
Axiology, xi-xii, 36-37, 39; change/ shift in, 47, 64-65, 83-84, 85-86; consensus in, 9-10, 42-43, 45-46, 47, 59-60; critiqued, 50-62, 103-104; dissensus in, 10-11, 12, 13, 16-17, 38, 41, 42-43, 44, 45-46, 47, 48, 49-50, 61-62, 63, 73; as emotive, 47-49; in hierarchical model, 26, 34-35, 47, 49; implicit v. explicit, 53-60, 62; of paradigms, 69-70, 74, 77-79, 80, 85; Popper on, 47, 48-49; realism on, 104-137; in reticulated model, 63; sociologists on, 44; theory and practice reconciled in, 50, 53-60, 61; utopian, 50, 51-53, 61

Bacon, Francis, 5, 81, 94
Bailly, J. S., 58
Barber, Bernard, 10
Barnes, Barry, 40
Beliefs, 28-29, 30
Berkeley, George, 56

Boerhaave, Hermann, 56, 113
Boscovich, Roger, 57, 58
Boyd, Richard, 104, 106, 109, 115, 117, 125, 126, 134, 137
Buffon, G. L., 56
Burian, Richard, 112

Campbell, N. R., 4
CER. See Realism, convergent epistemological
Certainty, in science, 83
Change, 4-5, 8, 12, 13-14, 16, 99-100, 103; axiological, 47, 64-65, 83-84, 85-86; holist view of, 68-74, 80-81, 82, 83, 84-85, 86, 87; methodological, 57, 58-59, 81-83, 84, 85, 95-96; paradigm, 69-70, 72, 74, 76-80, 82-83, 84, 95
Chemistry: aether theories in, 113-114; Priestley-Dalton-Lavoisier controversy in, 13, 72-73, 88-89, 99-100, 101; referential theories in, 111
Choice: factual, 26-33, 35, 38; theory, 28-33, 89-91; underdetermination in, 27, 28-30, 31, 32, 33
Cognitive values. See Axiology
Collins, Harry, 21, 30

145

Communism, 9
Concomitant variations, 81, 94
Condillac, Étienne de, 56
Consensus, 3-13, 20, 86; axiological, 9-10, 42-43, 45-46, 47, 59-60; factual, 23-33, 41, 43, 44, 45, 46; formation, 2, 6, 16, 17, 18, 21, 23-41, 43, 73-74, 80, 87 (*see also* Hierarchical model of justification; Reticulated model of justification); Kuhn on, 14, 17-18, 19; methodological, 12, 33-41, 45, 46; philosophers on, 44; Polanyi on, 10, 12; in theory preference, 89-91; on world-view, 76-77
Consistency, 53-55, 91, 92-95
Contact action, 60, 61
Continental drift theory, 13, 28, 123
Convergence. *See* Realism, convergent epistemological
Copernicans, v. Ptolemaists, 7-8, 10-11, 13
Correspondence, 53, 116, 121, 122, 123, 124-126
Covariance fallacy, 43-50, 96
Creationism, 13, 29

Dalton, John, 7, 72-73, 99-100, 101
Darwin, Charles, 81
Deduction. *See* Hypothesis
Descartes, René, 94; physics of, 60-61, 65, 80
Dewey, John, 40, 83
Difference, 81, 94
Disinterestedness, 9
Dissensus, 2, 3, 7-8, 13-22, 93; axiological, 10-11, 12, 13, 16-17, 38, 41, 42-43, 44, 45-46, 47, 48, 49-50, 61-62, 63, 73; factual, 6, 23-24, 25, 26-33, 41, 43, 44, 73; interparadigmatic, 14, 16, 18-19, 72-73, 76, 79-80, 81-82, 83, 86-87, 95-96, 97, 101, 102; methodological, 25-26, 33-35, 36-38, 39-

40; in philosophy, 4, 9-10; in science, 4, 9-10; in theory preference, 89-91
Doppelt, Gerald, 95, 99, 100, 101, 102
Duheim-Quine thesis, 15
Duhem, Pierre, 127

Egalitarianism, cognitive, 30
Empiricism, logical, 1, 2, 7-8, 12
Energetics, 13
Epistemology, 39-41, 103. *See also* Realism, convergent epistemological; Relativism, epistemic
Ethics, xi-xii
Euler, Leonhard, 58
Evolution, theory of, 13, 29

Factual: choices, 26-33, 35, 38; consensus, 23-33, 41, 43, 44, 45, 46; dissensus, 6, 23-24, 25, 26-33, 41, 43, 44, 73
Fallibilism, 51-52, 83, 84
Falsification, 19
Feyerabend, Paul, xiii, 13, 16, 19, 20, 22
Foucault, Jean B. L., 68, 74, 86
Franklin, Benjamin, 56

Grünbaum, Adolf, 129
Gutting, Gary, 26 n. 3

Hartley, David, 57, 58, 114
Helmholtz, Hermann von, 81
Hempel, Carl, 67
Herschel, J. F. William, 59, 94 .
Hertz, G., 81
Hierarchical model of justification, 23-41, 77-78, 83; axiological level of, 26, 34-35, 47, 49; breaks down, 42-43; v. Kuhn's, 69-70; replaced, 62, 73
Holist model of scientific change, 68-74, 80-81, 82, 83, 84-85, 86, 87

Hooker, Clifford, 127
Hume, David, 56, 81, 134
Hypothesis: v. induction, 57, 58-59, 81-82; method of (hypothetico-deduction), 57-59, 81-82; realism as, 135, 136

Incommensurability, 13, 14-20, 34, 67, 86, 101
Induction, 55-56; v. hypothesis, 57, 58-59, 81-82; inference in, 59, 81
Infallibilism, 51-52, 83, 84
Inference, inductive, 59, 81
Instrumentalism, v. realism, 45, 48, 104, 135
Instrumental rationality theory. *See* Hierarchical model of justification
Intelligibility, 60-61, 84

Justification. *See* Hierarchical model of justification; Reticulated model of justification

Kepler, Johann, 32
Keynes, John Maynard, 36
Koertge, Noretta, 125
Krajewski, W., 121, 122, 125, 131
Kuhn, Thomas, xiv, 13; breaks with positivism, 69-70; challenge of, 67; clarifies theses, 67-68, 70; on consensus, 14, 17-18, 19; on consistency, 91-92; criticism of, 17, 68, 70-71, 72, 73; holist view of change of, xiii, 68-74, 80-81, 83, 84-85, 86, 87; on incommensurability, 14-20, 67, 86; on inter-paradigmatic dissensus, 14, 16, 18-19; on local underdetermination, 88-102; on methodology, 30-31, 32, 87-102; on normal science, 17; on quasi-shared values, 81 n. 12, 85; paradigm concept of, 17, 43-44, 47, 68-70, 71, 72,

73-74, 79-80, 95; on scientific rationality, xii-xiii

Lakatos, Imre, 19-20, 49, 68, 74, 87
Laplace, Pierre de, 113
Laudan, Larry, 68
Lavoisier, A. L., 72-73, 88-89, 113
Leibnizian ideal, 5-6, 7, 8, 11, 14, 22, 24-25, 33
Lesage, George, 57, 58-59, 114
Lugg, Andrew, 25 n. 2

Mach, Ernst, 81, 127
McMullin, Ernan, 125
Maxwell, J. C., 114
Merton, Robert, 1, 9-10, 11, 12, 16
Methodology/methodological rules, 5, 7, 8, 9, 11, 43, 48, 49; ambiguity in, 15, 29, 30-31, 32, 89-90, 91, 92, 94; change/shift in, 57, 58-59, 81-83, 84, 85, 95-96; confirms theory, 6; consensus in, 12, 33-41, 45, 46; as constraint, 24; dissensus in, 25-26, 33-35, 36-38, 39-40; function of, 34; inconsistency in, 92-95; Kuhn on, 30-31, 32, 87-102; mediated by axiology, 35-37; of paradigms, 69-70, 74, 77-79, 80, 85; problem-weighting in, 96-102; realist, 105; underdetermination of, 35-36, 39-40, 44; solves factual disagreements, 24-25, 26-33
Mill, John Stuart, 5, 36, 94
Miller, David, 131-132
Mitroff, Ian, 16
Mulkay, Michael, 20

Nagel, Ernest, 34, 45, 67
Newton, Isaac, 56, 59, 81, 94; v. Aristotle, 31-32; v. Kepler, 32; physics of, 31-32, 60-61, 65, 80
Newton-Smith, William, 106, 108, 119, 134, 137

Niiniluoto, Ilkka, 131
Norms, Merton's, 9-10, 11, 12. *See also* Axiology

Ontology, of paradigms, 68-69, 74, 77-79, 80, 85. *See also* Factual
Optics, wave-particle, 7

Paradigm: articulation, 73-74; axiologies of, 69-70, 74, 77-79, 80, 85; change/shift, 69-70, 72, 74, 76-80, 82-83, 84, 95; consensus, 76-77; inseparability of, 71; Kuhn's concept of, 17, 43-44, 47, 68-70, 71, 72, 73-74, 79-80, 95; meanings of, 68-69; methodologies of, 69-70, 74, 77-79, 80, 85; ontologies of, 68-69, 74, 77-79, 80, 85; self-authenticating, 17
Peirce, Benjamin, 36, 81, 83
Philosophy: consensus in, 44; dissensus in, 4, 9-10; on/of science, 1-2, 3-4, 5-8, 9, 11, 12, 16, 21-22, 44, 47, 48, 67, 103
Physics: aether theories in, 113-114, 129; Aristotelian, 31-32; Cartesian, 13, 60-61, 65, 80; limiting cases in, 129, 130; Newtonian, 31-32, 60-61, 65, 80
Placebo effect, 38-39
Planck principle, 18
Poincaré, J. H., 127
Polanyi, Michael, 10, 12
Popper, Karl, 1, 8, 33, 36, 67, 104, 124, 125, 131; on scientific goals, 47, 48-49
Positivism, 69-70, 115
Post, Heinz, 125, 131
Predesignation, 36
Priestley, Joseph, 72-73, 88-89
Ptolemaists, 7-8, 10-11, 13
Putnam, Hilary, 104, 106, 108, 119, 122, 124, 125, 126, 127, 130, 132, 134, 137; on reference, 109-110, 111, 112-113, 114, 117

Quine, W. V. O., 15, 39-40 n. 14

Rationality. *See* Hierarchical model of justification; Scientific rationality
Realism: on axiologies, 104-137; convergent epistemological, 105-109, 115-116, 117, 118, 121, 122, 123, 125, 128, 129, 130, 131, 132, 134; as hypothesis, 135, 136; intentional, 105; v. instrumentalism, 45, 48, 104, 135; methodology in, 105; semantic, 105; scientific, 104-137
Reference, 107, 108, 134; in chemistry, 111; Putnam on, 109-110, 111, 112-113, 114, 117; and success in science, 109-117, 120-121, 123, 124, 136
Reichenbach, Hans, 47, 49
Relativism, 47 n. 2, 49-50; epistemic, 30, 104
Retentionism, 105, 107, 116, 124-125, 126-127, 131-132
Reticulated model of justification, 62-66, 73, 79-80; axiology in, 63; constraints in, 63, 64; mutuality in, 62-63
Rumford, Benjamin, 113

Sampling, 38
Science: analogy in, 58, 59; approximate truth in, 117-120, 134, 136; change/revolution in, 4-5, 8, 12, 13-14, 46, 64, 65, 70-80, 82-87, 99-100, 103; correspondence in, 53, 116, 121, 122, 123, 124-125; counternormal behavior in, 13, 16; crisis, 17-18; as cumulative, 8; decision-making models in, 5-22; demarcation of, 2; epistemology in, 103; falsification in, 19; immature, 121, 122; incommensurability in, 13-20, 34, 67, 86, 101; induction in, 55-56, 57,

58, 59; intelligible, 60-61, 84; limiting cases in, 107, 108, 121, 124-125, 126, 127, 128, 130, 132, 136; mature, 81, 106, 107, 108, 109, 114, 121-122, 124, 130-131, 132; normal, 17-18, 19; observable v. unobservable entities in, 23, 55-59, 81; philosophy of/on, 1-2, 3-4, 5-8, 9, 11, 12, 16, 21-22, 44, 47, 48, 67, 103; progress in, 64-66, 107-108; as quest for certainty, 83; retention in, 105, 107, 116, 124-125, 126-127, 131-132; sociology of/on, 1-2, 3-4, 9-12, 16, 20, 21-22, 44; success in, 107-108, 109-117, 120-121, 122, 123, 124, 132-133, 134, 135, 137; verisimilitude in, 117-120, 134. *See also* Axiology; Consensus; Dissensus; Methodology
Scientific method. *See* Methodology/methodological rules
Scientific rationality, xii-xiii, 3, 41, 47, 48, 63, 64
Scientific realism, 104-137
Sellars, Wilfrid, 104, 109, 125, 132
Skepticism, organized, 9, 11 n. 3
Sociology: on axiology, 44; dissensus in, 4, 9-10; norms of, 9-19;

on/of science, 1-2, 3-4, 9-12, 16, 20, 21-22, 44
Success: and approximate truth, 117-118, 119, 120-124, 133, 136; in science, 107-108, 109-117, 120-121, 122, 123, 124, 132-133, 134, 135, 137
Szumilewicz, I., 125-126

Testing, 25, 39
Toulmin, Stephen, 68

Underdetermination, 13, 15-16, 84-85, 86; of factual choices, 27, 28-30, 31, 32, 33; Kuhn on, 88-102; local, 88-102; in methodology, 35-36, 39-40, 44; of theories, 27, 87-88
Universalism, 9
Utopianism, 50, 51-53, 61

Values. *See* Axiology
Verisimilitude, 117-120, 134

Watkins, John, 124-125, 127, 131
Whewell, William, 59, 80, 81, 125

Ziman, John, 4
Zuckerman, Harriet, 9

Designer:	UC Press Staff
Compositor:	Janet Sheila Brown
Printer:	Vail-Ballou
Binder:	Vail-Ballou
Text:	Baskerville 11/13
Display:	Baskerville